Collins Complete Energy-saving DIY

Collins
complete
energy-
saving
DIY

Albert Jackson and David Day

Collins

Collins Complete Energy-saving DIY
was originally created for HarperCollins Publishers by
Inklink/Jackson Day Jennings. Most of the material in
this book also appears in *Collins Complete DIY Manual*.

This new edition first published in 2008 by
Collins, an imprint of
HarperCollinsPublishers
77-85 Fulham Palace Road
Hammersmith
London W6 8JB

Collins is a registered trademark
of HarperCollins Publishers Ltd

13   12   11   10   09   08
6   5   4   3   2   1

A catalogue record for this book is available from
The British Library

ISBN 978 0 00 726672 2

Colour reproduction by Colourscan, Singapore
Printed and bound by Butler and Tanner, Frome

PLEASE NOTE
**Great care has been taken to ensure that the
information contained in Collins Complete Energy-
saving DIY is accurate. However, the law concerning
Building Regulations, planning, local bylaws and
related matters is neither static nor simple. A book
of this nature cannot replace specialist advice in
appropriate cases and therefore no responsibility
can be accepted by the publishers or by the authors
for any loss or damage caused by reliance upon the
accuracy of such information.**

**If you live outside Britain, your local conditions
may mean that some of this information is not
appropriate. If in doubt, always consult a qualified
electrician, plumber or surveyor.**

Mixed Sources
Product group from well-managed
forests and other controlled sources
www.fsc.org Cert no. SW-COC-1806
© 1996 Forest Stewardship Council
FSC

FSC is a non-profit international organisation established to promote the
responsible management of the world's forests. Products carrying the FSC
label are independently certified to assure consumers that they come
from forests that are managed to meet the social, economic and
ecological needs of present and future generations.

Find out more about HarperCollins and the environment at
www.harpercollins.co.uk/green

Authors
Albert Jackson and David Day

Photographers
Airedale/David Murphy
Colin Bowling
Paul Chave
Ben Jennings
Neil Waving

Consultants
George Baxter
Roger Bisby
John Dees

Contributors
David Bridle

Design
Keith Miller
Elizabeth Standley

New Illustrations
Graham Edwards
Graham White

Illustrations
Robin Harris

Editors
Peter Leek
Barbara Dixon

Proofreader and Indexer
Mary Morton

Acknowledgements
The authors and publishers would like to thank the following
companies and individuals who supplied images:

6 Alan Weintraub/Arcaid/Corbis TL, Mark Bolton/Corbis BL,
Fernando Bengoechea/Beateworks/Corbis CR; 7 Alan
Marsh/Design Pics/Corbis; 8 Friedhelm Thomas/Elizabeth
Whiting Associates; 9 The Velux Co L, Walter
Geiersperger/Corbis TR, Jupiter Images CR; 10 Evergreener CL,
Honeywell BL; 11 Albert Jackson; 12 Danfoss Randall Ltd BL,
Andrea Rugg Photography/Beateworks/Corbis TR; 13 Ned
Frisk Photography/Corbis B, Nokia TR; 14 Bloomimage/Corbis
TL, Tetra Images/Corbis CL, Interflush B; 20 The Original Box
Sash Window Company Ltd BL, G E Fabbri C; 24 Own Label
Products TL; 25 Ciga; 26 Thermawrap TR; 36 Ikea TL, Ring
Lighting CL; 44 Opella Ltd CR; 45 Screwfix TR; 49 Ideal
Standard C, CR; Aqualisa Products Ltd BR; 50 Ideal Standard
TL; 51 Mira Showers BL; 52 Albion Water Heaters Ltd; 53
Rayotec Ltd; 54 Solartwin; 60 Myson

Contents

Energy-saving DIY

Introduction

There are very few people in the world who do not accept the need for action on climate change. Even in this country we have experienced sustained weather patterns that were rare just a few decades ago. In summer there have been record temperatures and drought, and serious flooding can occur at almost any time of year. Positive measures have to be taken on a global scale to change our future for the better, but also we are being encouraged as individuals to make a contribution towards energy efficiency in our homes.

What do we mean by energy and by energy efficiency?

People spout on about energy saving as if it were something we could bottle or put in the bank. It is a rather nebulous term that can mean a great many things. Electricity is perhaps the most familiar form of energy that all of us consume in our homes. But when we talk about using less electricity, what we are really

aiming at is a saving in the fuels that are used to generate that power. Similarly, when we do our best to prevent heat escaping from our homes, we are attempting to conserve the stocks of gas and oil that will one day run out.

No one wants to do without the benefits of modern living that we derive from consuming gas, oil and electricity – but if we make investments in insulation and draughtproofing, for example, we can enjoy the same levels of comfort at less cost to the environment. In other words, we are being more energy-efficient. Similarly, if we operate and control our central-heating systems with more care, we are able to reduce the amount of fuel we burn without feeling any discomfort. Energy efficiency has more to do with careful management of resources than with having to do without home comforts.

SEE ALSO > Insulation and ventilation 15–32, Efficient heating 55–68

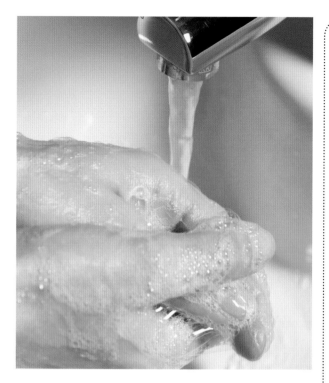

Why save water?

That is a reasonable question when we live in a country that seems to get more than its fair share of rain. Try convincing householders up to their knees in floodwater that they shouldn't use a hosepipe next time they want to water the garden. Unfortunately, when we experience such variations in weather, it can be difficult to appreciate the fuller picture. The truth is, despite the downpours, we have experienced summer after summer of comparative drought, and there is no reason at the moment to assume this won't continue. To enjoy the quality of water that is piped into our homes, all of us have to pay a great deal of money for purification and maintenance of the system. So, if nothing else, it makes economic sense to reduce unnecessary wastage however we can.

Living in the real world

The last thing this book aims to do is preach to you about your duty to do something about climate change. It is a book that seeks to offer simple advice with instructions on how you can repair, maintain and improve your home and, in so doing, reduce your fuel bills. You will, incidentally, be doing your bit towards mitigating the effects of global warming.

We also have to acknowledge that it is simply not possible for everyone to bring their homes up to the standards recommended by government agencies. Older homes, of which there are many thousands in this country, were built with different criteria than those used today. We can do a great deal to make them more energy-efficient, but not to the extent of destroying irreparably the charm and historic value of our unique housing stock.

Most of us can turn down the heating a degree or two without noticing the difference, but elderly home owners and residents require a higher ambient temperature just to feel tolerably warm.

We live in a world where aspirations and realities have to be balanced. You will find measures suggested in this book that can make a difference to your budget and help the environment without you having to make unacceptable sacrifices.

Financial assistance

The government and local authorities fund schemes to encourage home owners and tenants renting from private landlords to make energy-saving improvements to their houses and flats.

What sort of work is covered by the schemes?

Depending on your circumstances, there are grants to help with loft and cavity-wall insulation, installation of reflective radiator panels and thermostatic valves, draughtproofing, jackets for hot-water cylinders and compact fluorescent light bulbs. You may even be eligible for a complete new central-heating system or repairs to your existing system. Financial assistance is also provided to install a condensing boiler when your old boiler breaks down.

Who is eligible?

Most current schemes are available only to those who are receiving benefits, though people over a certain age may be entitled to free home improvements. The exact criteria are subject to changes from time to time – so if you think you may be eligible, contact your local authority for advice.

The work usually has to be carried out by approved contractors, and you will need to obtain an estimate from one of these contractors before funds can be made available. At the moment, there are no grants available for DIY improvements.

Who is providing the funds?

Government funding provides up to a maximum of £2700 to improve heating and energy efficiency. In most cases, you will only be eligible for a proportion of the estimated costs of these improvements. In England, the scheme is known as *Warm Front*. Similar schemes and funding are available in other parts of the UK: *Warm Homes* in Northern Ireland, *Warm Deal* and the *Central Heating Programme* in Scotland, and the *Home Energy Efficiency Scheme* in Wales.

Local authorities operate schemes under various names. Information can be obtained from your local council, who will usually provide application forms and leaflets that describe their particular schemes in detail.

Energy-supply companies are obliged by law to achieve certain targets for saving energy in the domestic market. As a result, suppliers provide a range of offers aimed at reducing energy consumption. They will either send a representative to your home to access what improvements you can make, or will ask you to provide information about your property that will allow them to suggest which measures will be of benefit and what grants are available to carry out the work. You can take up offers from any supply company, regardless of who actually supplies you with gas or electricity.

The internet is a useful source of information on obtaining funds towards energy-saving measures. Local authorities have their own websites that offer help to residents in their areas. The following websites may prove helpful for guidance on how to obtain the grants outlined above:
www.warmfrontgrants.co.uk
www.energysavingtrust.org.uk

See the following chapter for more information on how to get advice on grants for insulation.

• **Grants for renewable energy**
Householders can apply for sums of up to £2500 towards the installation of wind turbines and solar panels. For details, visit **www.lowcarbonbuildings. org.uk/home**

SEE ALSO > Energy conservation and older buildings 11, Insulation and ventilation 15–32, Conserving power and water 33–54, Thermostats 34, 61, Compact fluorescent tubes 36–7

New building work

With every project you undertake to extend or improve your home, there will be different criteria to consider and problems to solve. And no doubt architects and builders will take different views about how best to design an extension or conversion to make them energy-efficient as well as pleasant to live in. It can be a delicate balance to strike – often requiring practical solutions and compromises that you may not have considered in order to achieve your goals.

Food for thought

Cost is always a consideration, but the cheapest route may not necessarily be the most cost-effective in terms of long-term energy efficiency. These are aspects you need to discuss in detail with your professional advisors. The following suggestions are intended as pointers to the way you approach the design and build for the future.

Siting a new extension
If possible, locate a new extension on the side of the house where it can gain most from the effect of sunlight – often referred to as passive solar energy or solar gain. Try to incorporate ground-floor south-facing windows; and think about their height and proportion to maximize the winter sun's deeper penetration into your home, thereby absorbing free energy from the sun to help heat your home and reducing the need for electric illumination during the hours of daylight. You might want to consider a design that incorporates some form of shading above the windows that will prevent too much solar gain in the hotter summer months but admit maximum daylight in winter when the sun is lower in the sky.

Where possible it pays to install relatively small windows facing north, in order to reduce heat loss. Similarly, grouping wall storage on the north, east and west walls provides additional insulation.

Proportions
Consider the overall shape, size and layout of your extension or conversion. This can have a significant effect on thermal performance and building costs. For example, a simple cube may

be cheaper to construct than a long, thin rectangular shape. However, the latter could, in the right circumstances, provide a longer south-facing surface, which offers more scope for passive solar energy in the form of free sunlight and heat.

Within your design, think about having an open-plan layout, with the minimum number of door openings. One room or living space is easier to heat than several individual rooms. Lightweight stud partitions are the norm for dividing up internal spaces, especially upstairs; but talk to your designer or architect about incorporating at least some internal walls built from dense masonry, which will absorb heat during the day and then radiate warmth back into the living spaces as the house cools down.

Buffer zones
Consider introducing buffer zones into the overall design. A porch, for example, serves as an airlock, reducing heat loss and providing extra insulation against draughts and cold. A glazed conservatory on the west wall of the house can harvest solar energy in the late afternoon, and provide useful space for drying clothes. A similar conservatory helps to delay night-time cooling of the interior.

Build tight, ventilate right
Take measures to reduce losses from draughts and air movement through the external fabric of your home. The aim is to make the building envelope as airtight as possible and then provide controllable ventilation. Good ventilation helps provide a comfortable and healthy environment by diluting or extracting moisture and pollutants – such as nitrogen oxides, carbon dioxide, tobacco smoke and house-dust mites – from within your home. The worst pollutant, moisture vapour, should be extracted from bathrooms and kitchens, which are its prime source.

Householders usually think of fitting extractor fans to provide adequate ventilation, but ordinary fans extract heat along with the pollutants. Think about whether a heat-recovery ventilator might be a better solution. These units remove heat from the air flowing out of the building and then use it to warm the fresh air moving in the opposite direction. It is possible to have a centrally placed heat-recovery unit that extracts stale air from the more heavily polluted areas of the home – which is also where most heat is generated – and reintroduce fresh warmed air into areas of the home that would benefit most.

Mechanical extraction systems have to be powered by electricity, but you could have your new house built around a passive stack ventilation – which works on the principle that natural convection will extract the relatively warm moist air from inside the building while at the same time drawing in fresh air through trickle vents mounted in the windows or outside walls. Once installed, this type of whole-house ventilation won't cost a penny to run.

SEE ALSO > Insulation and ventilation 15–32

Insulation

Installing adequate insulation is perhaps the most important measure you can take to minimize your energy requirements. There are a number of materials you can use, including glass fibre, mineral wool, polystyrene and cellulose (recycled paper insulation). In the near future there will be other natural materials to choose from, such as straw, hemp and wool. One advantage in using these materials is that they are produced locally and do not have to be imported. Plan ahead and build for the future by incorporating high levels of insulation.

Roof insulation is comparatively simple to install in an existing building, but installing wall insulation can be difficult if not impossible in some older houses. However, when building a new home or extension be sure to take full advantage of effective insulation, which is so easy to incorporate into the walls during construction. Minimize the potential for 'thermal bridges' – vulnerable areas in the external fabric where heat can travel easily to the outside. Make sure that insulation is continuous, eliminating cold spots where condensation could occur.

Floor insulation is essential in new building work and can be installed with comparative ease when compared with a similar exercise in an older property.

Roof construction

When designing the roof covering for a new extension or loft conversion, try to construct what is known as a warm-roof system, whereby the insulation is contained within the sloping roof. This allows spaces within the roof void to be kept warm and used as habitable space. It also avoids having to ventilate the roof void above an insulated ceiling, thus reducing draughts and heat loss.

Building materials

Where practicable, use timber as your prime building material. This is without doubt the 'greenest' structural material available, provided you can ensure the wood comes from certifiable sustained managed sources. It also has the advantage of being a beautiful material that is relatively easy to work.

In addition, consider using second-hand materials, such as used bricks and recycled steel. And look for building blocks made with a high content of granulated blast-furnace slag (check manufacturers' descriptions for details).

Rammed-earth construction is now a recognized means of building walls, though you would need a professional to check that the soil is suitable in the area where the building is to be constructed.

Take advantage of natural light

Every modern building or extension must be wired for light and power, but when given the opportunity, it makes sense to take

maximum advantage of natural light to illuminate dark corridors and landings. Conventional roof lights – windows built into the roof structure – is one solution, but many architects are recommending 'light pipes' to introduce daylight into the more inaccessible parts of a building. Essentially, daylight is gathered from outside (usually at roof level) and transferred down a highly reflective tube to a diffuser mounted on the ceiling. Some fittings include a ventilator and an electric light so that the same source is used to illuminate the interior at night.

Water conservation

For your new bathrooms and cloakrooms, choose slimline dual-flush sanitary ware that uses relatively little water to flush the WC. And why use drinking water to flush the toilet or wash your clothes, when there are viable options for collecting rainwater for such purposes? Large storage tanks buried below ground are used to collect rainwater that's shed from your roof. This harvested water is pumped directly to your toilet cisterns and, if you wish, to your washing machine. Being soft water, it is ideal for washing clothes. The costs of installing and running a system that recycles rainwater is considered by some environmentalists to be counterproductive; however, a number of local authorities are already insisting that building contractors include such systems in their plans for new housing developments.

If you can afford it, you could install a similar system that collects 'grey water' – water discharged from handbasins, baths and showers. Unlike rainwater, which is relatively pure, grey water requires a settlement tank and filtration. Water from your kitchen sink, which contains grease and other contaminants, is not suitable for reuse.

Heating systems

You have more options to choose from when deciding on a heating system for a new house. You can install concealed ducting that will distribute heated air to every room in the building. Electrically heated elements built into the structure will radiate heat gently across the entire floor surface. This type of installation is often used to heat extensions. Most people still opt for a conventional wet central-heating system, driven by a gas-fired or oil-burning boiler. If you have the option, choose a condensing boiler, which is more economical to run.

Solar energy

This is a much-disputed issue, but one which is definitely gaining popularity. You can hope to do little more than contribute to heating your water if you install solar panels on the roof of an existing house. However, by using photovoltaic cells in the form of roof tiles, you can safely cover a large area of a south-facing roof and thereby collect enough solar energy to recover a significant proportion of your electricity bill.

With a small outlay, you can install dedicated solar panels that are designed to power a single lamp in order to illuminate a shed, garage or porch. This seems an ideal way to provide illumination without having to run electrical cable the length of your garden.

Wind turbines

It may seem like an attractive proposition to harness the wind to provide electrical power in your home. However, unless you live in a rural area of the country, wind power is unlikely to make a measurable difference to your electricity bill. It might be worth erecting a turbine high up on a well-supported pole, but, even then, you would need to live on a fairly exposed site where wind speeds are fairly constant. You will need consent from your local authority before you install a wind turbine.

Websites
Useful websites include:

www.rainharvesting.co.uk (rainwater harvesting)

www.greengardener.co.uk/wormeries.htm (tiger-worm composting)

**www.nef.org.uk
www.est.org.uk** (solar power for heating and hot water)

www.bwea.com (wind turbines)

SEE ALSO > Is your present home energy-efficient? 10, Insulation and ventilation 15–32, Conserving power and water 33–54, Efficient heating 55–68

Is your present home energy-efficient?

If you are about to build a new house or extension, any architect or informed builder will offer help and advice on conserving energy and water, but most of us simply want to know what measures we can realistically take in the short term in our existing home.

Reducing waste

When working on your present home, try to build in programmes of energy efficiency as part of your overall scheme. Our expectations of comfort and convenience are such that we all require central heating, electric lighting and power to run our modern appliances. No one is suggesting we should do away with these modern conveniences, but it makes sense to protect the environment and reduce our personal expenses at the same time.

Reducing energy wastage is particularly difficult if you live in an older property. Not only will it be built without modern levels of insulation, but it may also be more difficult to bring it up to standard without compromising the essential character of your home.

Fitting draught excluders

Draughtproofing doors and windows is a relatively inexpensive yet highly effective way to reduce heat lost to the outside. And you may be surprised to discover that draughts can enter through power points, the junctions between skirting boards and floors, gaps in the floorboards, gaps between ceilings and walls, and around loft hatches. The aim should be to seal as many gaps as possible, but the degree of airtightness achievable will depend on the type of wall construction and finish, how well services have been installed, and the age and condition of windows and doors.

Reducing your use of electrical energy

One of the simplest ways to use less electricity is to replace at least some of your ordinary tungsten-filament light bulbs with low-energy compact fluorescent versions. These so-called long-life bulbs are relatively expensive to buy, but reduce costs in the long run. The Building Regulations now require you to take into consideration the use of low-energy lighting when designing conversions and extensions.

When planning your kitchen, pay particular attention to the design of freezers and refrigerators, and monitor how they are working. Their thermostats have a habit of failing, often causing such appliances to run continuously. If you place your fridge freezer close to a source of heat, such as a cooker, it will have to work harder to maintain the required temperature inside the cabinet.

Are you getting the best possible deal from your electricity and gas suppliers? It may pay to shop around.

Thermostats and time switches

These are important for regulating heating appliances. Thermostats prevent appliances from getting hotter than necessary, and time switches can be used to make sure the appliances are running only during specified periods.

Fit thermostatic radiator valves to your existing radiators. This allows you to control the temperature of each individual radiator to suit the particular conditions in the part of the house where it is situated. A thermostatic radiator valve will shut down a radiator as soon as it reaches the required temperature, thereby preventing heat being wasted in areas of the home where it is not required. These valves are relatively inexpensive and easy to fit.

Boilers and hot-water cylinders

At the moment, gas-fired central-heating systems are probably the most effective and efficient available, but this may change with fluctuations in the ever-volatile fuel markets.

The past few years have seen advances in efficient boilers and controls, so much so that the expense of replacing old worn-out equipment can often be recouped quickly in fuel savings. If you are replacing a boiler, choose an energy-efficient condensing boiler and make sure it is part of a well-designed heating system that allows the boiler to work in condensing mode most of the time.

Most hot-water storage cylinders are now supplied pre-insulated, having a layer of foam sprayed on the outside. However, a lot of houses are still plumbed with older uninsulated copper cylinders that waste considerable amounts of heat. Wrapping a proprietary insulating jacket around the cylinder will start to reduce your heating bills within just a few months.

Similarly, wrapping exposed hot-water pipes in foamed-plastic tubing is an inexpensive energy-saving measure. Look especially for pipes running through unheated areas of the house, such as the cellar and roof space.

Loft insulation

Wherever possible, increase the insulation in your roof space. This is where the majority of heat is lost. Remember that increased insulation may require better ventilation in order to prevent condensation forming in the roof timbers.

Reducing heat lost through doors and windows

When necessary, have replacement windows and doors made to a high standard. In terms of heat loss, the most efficient windows are large plain units without glazing bars (with every additional glazing bar there is more potential for heat loss). Similarly, the design of the window surround must be considered to maximize heat retention. Double-glazed units with large edge details transfer more heat than ones that utilize smaller sections. Most energy-efficient double-glazed units have an air gap of around 16mm (^{5}/8in) filled with argon gas and are made from low-emissivity glass. If you are replacing windows on the north or east elevations of your house, it is worth considering triple glazing.

Reducing your household water consumption

There are some very simple ways to reduce your water consumption, such as installing spray taps, self-closing taps and electronic-sensor taps, all of which reduce the amount of hot and cold water that is poured away needlessly.

It is perfectly feasible to collect rainwater and use it for watering the garden, or it can be filtered then stored for household use.

SEE ALSO ► Insulation and ventilation 15–32, Conserving power and water 33–54, Efficient heating 55–68

Energy conservation and older buildings

Energy efficiency comes within the scope of the Building Regulations, which are divided into various parts, each designated by a letter. Energy conservation is referred to as Part L, Conservation of Fuel and Power. The regulations apply to new buildings and to existing houses when they are altered, extended or subjected to a new use. However, Part L makes it clear that the special characteristics of a historic building must be recognized. The aim of this revised part of the Building Regulations is to improve energy efficiency where it is practical to do so.

For existing buildings, Part L (2002) generally requires energy-conservation upgrading only for elements that are to be 'substantially replaced' as part of the work. The requirements do not apply to general repairs or to elements that don't need replacing.

Where proposed alterations or replacements could trigger Part L of the Building Regulations, care must be exercised in deciding whether or not such work will affect the building's character. If your house is listed, listed-building consent may be required. In some instances, a historic building may be in an almost totally original state and like-for-like replacement will be the only appropriate solution. In many cases, however, some thermal upgrading may be practicable - for example, between the joists within roof spaces and under suspended floors – provided it doesn't pose technical problems, such as inhibiting ventilation. It may even be reasonable for this insulation to exceed the recommendations in Part L, in order to help make up for shortcomings elsewhere.

In terms of ventilation and moisture control, old houses can have quite different requirements from newer buildings. Houses built with solid walls without a damp-proof course and from permeable materials function differently from buildings constructed using modern standards and practices. As a result, these older buildings may require comparatively more ventilation to ensure their wellbeing. Nevertheless, a new extension to an old house will normally be expected to have a higher degree of thermal performance than the original building to which it is attached.

Energy Performance Certificates

Home Information Packs (HIPS) are intended to give potential buyers important information about a house they are thinking of purchasing, and contain an Energy Performance Certificate (EPC). This certificate rates a particular house or flat in terms of energy efficiency. In theory, it could affect the value of the property.

From December 2007 it has been mandatory for the seller of a house or flat of any size to present a potential buyer with a home information pack. The aim is to increase public awareness of issues that may not be obvious from casual inspection. Generally, we know whether we like the appearance of a house, its size, layout and location, but now we are also being offered information about things like energy consumption and potential fuel bills. It is hoped that this measure will increase public demand for energy-efficient buildings and encourage home owners and builders to invest in low-carbon measures.

In practice, vendors, through estate agents, need to employ a competent person to produce a certificate that rates the energy performance of their home from A to G, very much like the ratings you see on appliances such as fridges or washing machines. The certificate outlines the running costs and the effects on carbon emissions of space heating, hot water and lighting. It also gives practical advice on how to cut these costs and reduce emissions. The EPC forms part of the Home Information Pack, which also includes searches and other legal documents. The entire system is designed to tackle the uncertainty and lack of transparency in buying a house, and will hopefully lead to fewer failed transactions.

For more detailed information, visit **homeinformationpacks.gov.uk**.

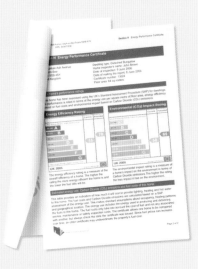

SEE ALSO > Insulation and ventilation 15–32

Simple ways to save energy

Having read this book, you will be aware of a great many DIY solutions to saving energy and water, but you can also make a difference to your electricity bills simply by changing your habits.

Switch off

Our parents and grandparents were brought up to switch off the light when they left a room, but nowadays we have got into the habit of leaving lights switched on all over the house. Train yourself and your family to switch off unnecessary lighting. You only need background illumination when watching TV; and once you have settled down for the evening, perhaps just one or two table lamps are all you need for reading or playing games.

Stand-by mode

Many electrical appliances such as TV sets and music systems can be left on 'stand-by', so they can be reactivated using a remote controller. The small lamp that indicates an appliance is in stand-by mode consumes an insignificant amount of electricity, but the cumulative effect represents wastage on a colossal scale. Unless you need to leave your equipment set up to record a programme on TV or radio, try to remember to turn off these appliances at the socket.

Turn the heating down

Turning down the thermostat by one degree can save a great deal of money, and you probably won't even notice the difference in comfort.

Why not turn off the radiators in spare bedrooms that are used infrequently? If you need gentle background heat in the room – to prevent condensation, for example – fit a thermostatically-controlled valve to the radiator.

Night lights and safety lighting

If you have children who are afraid to sleep in the dark, plug a special low-powered light fitting into a socket in their room. This is far more energy-efficient than leaving a light burning on the landing. A similar fitting can provide low-level illumination on a landing in case someone needs to use the bathroom during the night. If that is not a practical solution, can you leave a table lamp or uplighter plugged into a timer that will switch off the lamp at dawn?

Security lighting

Outdoor security lighting is essential if you want to identify a caller after dark. But don't install lighting that stays on permanently. Have a porch light that is activated by movement as the caller approaches the front door, and make sure the fitting has a dusk-to-dawn sensor that prevents the light coming on during daylight hours.

Boil less water

There is no need to fill the kettle each time you make a cup of tea or coffee. You can see the heating element inside older-style kettles and, provided there is enough water to cover the element, you can't do any harm. If the element is concealed in the base, get used to using the measurements marked on the kettle to avoid overfilling it. Make sure the lid is fitted properly or the kettle will continue to boil without switching off.

You have to cover potatoes with water to boil them properly in a saucepan, but you can cook a steamer full of other vegetables on top of the same saucepan.

SEE ALSO > Thermostats 34, 61

Cook more efficiently

Instead of using the grill or hob, as well as the oven, to cook food, plan some meals so that you can use your oven to cook vegetables and meat at the same time.

A fan oven heats up faster than a conventional one, so don't switch your fan oven on too soon in order to bring it up to the temperature recommended in your cookbook.

It can take as much as an hour to bake potatoes in the oven, but you can precook them in your microwave for about 10 minutes before putting them in your oven just to brown the skins.

Economize on laundry

Most modern washing machines and detergents provide the opportunity to do the laundry on a 'cool' or 'fast' programme, which saves considerably on electricity.

Electric tumble dryers are a real boon, especially in the winter months. However, if you have the space in the garden, or even a balcony, hanging your washing on a clothes line in warm and windy weather could save having to use your tumble dryer for up to 50 minutes per day.

Close your curtains

Fitting effective draught excluders is covered in the next chapter, but even draughtproofed windows can sap the warmth from a room. Close your curtains or blinds at dusk to reduce heat loss. Good-quality lined curtains work best, especially if there's a closed pelmet across the top of the window.

Buy and use appliances wisely

When buying new electrical appliances, look for labelling that provides information on their energy efficiency (see LOWER RUNNING COSTS). Also, choose appliances that suit your personal lifestyle. As a single person, you can probably function very well with energy-efficient compact fridges, dishwashers and ovens. Buy a slow cooker that uses a trickle of electricity during the day in order to have a meal ready when you get home.

A big family will use less energy and water by installing a large washing machine, instead of having to use a smaller appliance perhaps once or twice a day to keep up with the laundry.

Using an electric toaster every morning is more energy-efficient than switching on your cooker grill to toast the bread.

Use your mobile-phone alarm

A plug-in alarm radio beside you bed uses a small amount of electricity day and night, simply to illuminate the clock face. To wake you in the morning, use your mobile phone, which has an alarm facility that switches on the phone at the time you set. Alternatively, buy a simple battery-operated alarm clock.

Christmas illuminations

More and more we seem to be adopting the American custom of putting up extensive outdoor decorations at Christmas. It would be a pity to dispense with them altogether; but if you were to calculate the running cost of a house festooned with electric 'fairy' lights, you might think twice about it.

SEE ALSO > Draught excluders 18–20, Lower running costs 35

Simple ways to conserve water

As more and more homes are fitted with water meters, consumers are waking up to the fact that it makes as much sense to reduce water wastage as it does to cut back on consumption of gas and electricity.

Turn the tap off

Don't leave the tap running when you are brushing your teeth. Similarly, turn off the shower when you are rubbing shampoo into your hair or soaping your body.

Don't rinse vegetables and salad under a running tap. Run some cold water into a bowl, then rinse the salad first before scrubbing soil off the vegetables in the same water.

Never wash crockery under a running hot tap.

When we want a drink of cool water, most of us run off the water standing in the pipe until colder water begins to flow. Cut back on waste by keeping a jug of drinking water in the fridge.

Fill the dishwasher before using it

Only very large families are likely to fill the average dishwasher after every meal. Don't be tempted to run a full programme with a machine that is only half full. Put it on a rinse cycle only to prevent odours from food particles left drying on the dishes, then complete the job after your next meal. This not only uses less water but reduces your electricity consumption, too.

Don't overfill your bath

There is no need to emulate movie actresses who sit up to their neck in foaming baths. In the real world, you can take a bath in water that is deep enough to covers your legs.

Don't leave just the hot tap running when you are filling a bath. You'll only waste more water cooling it down again. The best option is a mixer tap set to run water at just the right temperature from the start.

Use less water when flushing the WC

Whenever possible, fit a new slimline dual-flush cistern to your WC. These cisterns hold half the water contained in the older style 8–12 litre models. By pressing the relevant buttons that operate the dual-flush mechanism, you can decide to instigate half or full flush.

Alternatively, fit a mechanism to your lever-operated cistern that will reconfigure the standard siphon-flushing system. Normally, when you depress and then release the lever, the entire contents of the cistern is used to flush the WC. Once the 'interflush' mechanism is fitted, you hold down the lever until the pan is empty. At that point, you release the lever and flushing stops – reducing the amount of water used to precisely what is needed each time.

In the past, placing a house brick in the bottom of the cistern was often recommended as a way to reduce the capacity of an overlarge cistern. The modern equivalent is known as a 'hippo', which can best be described as a flexible open-ended plastic box that you fit into an old-style cistern, just below the float. Once the hippo is full of water, it sinks to the bottom of the cistern, where it remains, reducing the capacity of the cistern, and therefore the amount of water flushed, by about 3 litres.

Save water in the garden

The fact that we have come to expect hosepipe bans in the height of summer should tell us something about the amount of water we pour onto our gardens. There are a number of ways we can reduce that expenditure without it having a detrimental effect on the plants.

Banish the sprinkler

First and foremost, don't use a sprinkler to water the lawn. Instead, adjust your mower to leave the grass longer in the hotter weather, so that the roots do not dry out as fast. Grass is very hardy and will recover from the driest conditions we can expect in this country.

Choose the best time to water plants

Avoid watering in the heat of the day when moisture evaporates faster, leaving less water for the plants to absorb. A layer of mulch spread in your flowerbeds will help to retain the moisture. Water larger shrubs and plants less often. Their root systems will find moisture deeper underground.

Watering cans and hosepipes

In a small garden, you can use a watering can to water the plants. This is definitely the best way to water window boxes and containers. If you must use a hosepipe, fit a trigger-operated nozzle, so water is not wasted as you move the hose from one location to another.

The very best option is to install a water butt that collects rainwater. Some butts have a tap from which to fill a watering can, or you can install a small pump to deliver the water to a hosepipe.

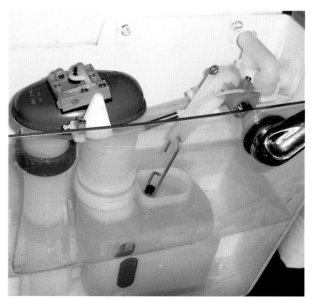

Fit a mechanism that helps control the amount of water you use to flush the WC.

SEE ALSO > Simple ways to save energy 12–13, Collecting waste water 38, Mixers taps 47, 50, Maintaining cisterns and storage tanks 44–5

Insulation
and ventilation

Energy in the form of heat simply leaks away from an uninsulated house. A colossal 60 per cent of the lost heat escapes through the roof and walls, and another 25 per cent through unsealed doors and windows. Add to that total the heat wasted from uninsulated floors, single-glazed windows and unlagged hot-water cylinders and you begin to appreciate the scale of the problem.

Campaigns alerting us to the need for effective insulation have been going for a long time now. So much so, there must be few homes where insulation has not been tackled to some extent already. However, recommended levels of insulation have increased substantially over the past few years, so it would pay to check whether your present insulation comes up to standard.

Adequate insulation is a good investment and your outlay should be recouped in fuel savings within two to three years. If you qualify for a government or local-authority grant, the payback period is even shorter.

Ventilation is included in this chapter in order to avoid possible adverse consequences of insulation, such as condensation and wood rot.

Insulating your home

No matter what fuel you use, the cost of heating a home continues to rise. Saving money is a major consideration – but of equal importance is the need to conserve energy in order to protect the environment. Even if such considerations could be ignored, the improved comfort and health of your family would more than justify the effort and expense of installing or upgrading insulation in your home.

Insulation grants

Because home insulation is of benefit to the economy, the government has made discretionary grants available through its *Warm Front* scheme to encourage people to insulate and draughtproof their houses and flats. However, the work has to be carried out by professional contractors, and these grants are not available at present for DIY insulation.

To find out whether you are eligible for a grant and how to process your application, phone the following numbers. If your home is in England, call 0800 316 6011. In Scotland, call 0800 316 1653. In Wales, call 0800 316 2815. In Northern Ireland, call 0800 181 667.

• **Kelvin**
Kelvin is used as a measurement of the difference between one temperature and another, whereas Celsius is used to define the difference between zero and a given temperature.

Specifications

When comparing thermal insulating materials, you are likely to encounter certain technical specifications.

U-values

Elements of a building's structure and the insulation itself are often assigned a U-value. This indicates the rate at which heat is transmitted from one side of a wall or ceiling, for example, to the other. It is measured in watts per square metre per degree kelvin (W/m²k).

For example, if a solid brick wall is specified as having a U-value of 2.0, it means that 2 watts of heat are conducted from every square metre of the wall for every degree difference in the temperature on each side of the wall. If the temperature outside is 10 degrees lower than inside, each square metre of the wall will conduct 20 watts of heat. The lower the U-value, the better the insulation.

R-values

A material may be given an R-value, which indicates the resistance to heat flow of a specified thickness. Materials with superior insulating qualities have the highest R-values.

Deciding on your priorities

Opinion differs on the exact figures, but it is estimated that from the average uninsulated house 35 per cent of the lost heat escapes through the walls, 25 per cent through the roof, 25 per cent through draughty doors and windows, and 15 per cent through the floor. At best, this is no more than a rough guide, as it is difficult to define an 'average' home in order to estimate the rate of heat loss. A terraced house, for example, will lose less than a detached house of identical size, even though their roofs have the same area and are in similar condition. And other factors are relevant, too – for instance, large ill-fitting sash windows permit far greater heat loss than tightly fitting casements.

Although these statistics identify the major routes for heat loss, they do not necessarily indicate where you should begin your insulation programme in order to achieve the quickest return on your investment – or, for that matter, the most immediate improvement in terms of comfort. In fact, it is best to start with relatively inexpensive measures.

1 Hot-water cylinder and pipes
Modern cylinders are manufactured with an outer layer of foam insulation, but if you have one of the older uninsulated cylinders you should begin by lagging it with a segmented mineral-fibre jacket. At the same time, lag the hot-water pipes that run through unheated areas of your house. These simple measures will constitute a considerable saving in a matter of only a few months.

2 Radiators
Fit a foil-faced lining behind radiators against external walls. This will reflect heat back into the room, instead of it being absorbed by the wall.

3 Draughtproofing
Eliminate heat loss around all windows and doors, including draughts between sliding sashes. In return for a modest outlay, draughtproofing helps reduce heating costs and provides increased comfort. It is also easy to accomplish.

4 Roof
Tackle the insulation of your roof next. Most householders will have installed loft insulation at some time, but in most cases the level of insulation will not be adequate to meet current recommended standards and if possible should be topped up.

5 Walls
Depending on the construction of your house, insulating the walls may be a sound investment. However, it's likely to be a relatively expensive operation and, unless you qualify for a substantial grant towards the cost of installation, it may take several years for you to recoup your initial outlay.

6 Floors
Floorcoverings such as carpets, tiles or parquet offer some degree of insulation. Whether you install extra insulation is likely to depend on the level of comfort you require, and also on whether you need to carry out other improvements to a floor. Floor insulation is a mandatory requirement for all new dwellings.

7 Double glazing
Contrary to the typical advertisements, double glazing will produce only a slow return on your investment, especially if you choose one of the more expensive glazing systems. However, it may help to increase the value of your property, and a double-glazed room is definitely cosier. In addition, you will be troubled by less noise from outside, especially if you choose to install triple glazing.

SEE ALSO ▷ Grants 7, Draughtproofing 18–20, Insulating roofs 21–4, Insulating walls 25–6, Insulating floors 26, Double glazing 27–9

Lagging pipes, cylinders and radiators

Some very effective measures, such as lagging the hot-water pipes and cylinder, are so simple they can be undertaken by householders who have had little practical do-it-yourself experience.

Insulating the cylinder

People used to think that an unlagged cylinder had the advantage of providing a useful source of heat in an airing cupboard – but in fact it squanders a surprising amount of energy. Even a lagged cylinder should provide ample heat in an enclosed airing cupboard; if not, an uninsulated pipe will do so.

Buying a water-cylinder jacket
Proprietary water-cylinder jackets are made from segments of mineral-fibre insulation, 75 to 100mm (3 to 4in) thick, wrapped in plastic. Measure the approximate height and circumference of the cylinder to choose the right size.

If need be, buy a jacket that is too large, rather than one that is too small. Make sure the quality is adequate by checking that it is marked with the British Standard Kite mark.

Fitting a jacket
Thread the tapered ends of the jacket segments onto a length of string and tie it round the pipe at the top of the cylinder. Distribute the segments evenly around the cylinder, then wrap the straps round it to hold the jacket in place. Don't pull the straps too tight. Spread out the segments to make sure the edges are butted together, and tuck the insulation around the pipes and the thermostat. Check that the cable running to the immersion heater is not trapped between the insulation and the cylinder.

Wrap foamed-plastic tubes (see above right) around the pipework, especially the vent pipe directly above the cylinder.

If you should ever have to replace the cylinder itself, consider substituting a preinsulated version.

Lagging pipe runs

You should insulate hot-water pipes in those parts of the house where their radiant heat is not contributing to the warmth of the rooms, and cold-water pipes in unheated areas of the building (where they could freeze). You can wrap pipework in lagging bandages (there are several types, some of which are covered in reflective foil), but it is generally more convenient to use foamed-plastic tubes designed for the purpose. This is especially true for pipes close to a wall, which may be awkward to wrap.

Foamed-plastic tubes are produced to fit pipes of different diameters: the foamed plastic varies in thickness from 12 to 20mm (½ to ¾in). The more expensive ones incorporate a metallic-foil backing that reflects some of the heat back into hot-water pipes.

Most tubes are preslit along their length, so that they can be sprung over the pipe (**1**). Butt successive lengths of tube end-to-end, and seal the joints with PVC adhesive tape.

At a bend, cut small segments out of the split edge, so that it bends without crimping. Fit it around the pipe (**2**) and seal the closed joints with tape. If two pipes are joined with an elbow fitting, mitre the ends of the two lengths of tube, then butt them together (**3**) and seal with tape. Cut lengths of tube to fit snugly around a T-joint, linking them with a wedge-shaped butt joint, and seal with tape.

1 Spring onto pipe

2 Cut to fit a bend

3 Cut mitres for elbows

Reflecting heat from a radiator

As much as 25 per cent of the radiant heat from a radiator placed against an outside wall is lost to the wall behind it. You can reclaim maybe half this wasted heat by applying a foil-faced expanded-polystyrene lining to the wall behind the radiator, to reflect the heat back into the room. The material is available as rolls, sheets or tiles. It is easiest to apply the lining to the wall when the radiator is removed for decorating, but you can do it with the radiator in place.

Turn off the radiator and measure it, making a note of the position of the brackets. Use a sharp trimming knife or scissors to cut the lining to size, so it is slightly smaller than the radiator all round. Cut narrow slots, as need be, to fit over the fixing brackets (**1**).

Apply heavy-duty fungicidal wallpaper paste to the back of the material, and then slide it behind the radiator (**2**). Smooth it onto the wall with a wooden batten or a small roller used for painting radiators. Allow the paste to dry before turning the radiator on again. Alternatively, you can fix the lining in place with double-sided adhesive pads.

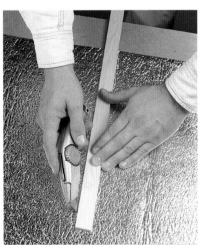

1 Cut slots to align with the wall brackets

2 Slide the lining behind the radiator

SEE ALSO > Grants 7, Hot-water cylinders 52–3

Draughtproofing

A certain amount of ventilation is desirable to maintain a healthy environment and keep condensation at bay; it's also essential to enable some heating appliances to operate properly and safely. However, uncontrolled draughts are hardly an efficient way to ventilate a house – and besides accounting for quite a large proportion of the heat lost, they cause a good deal of discomfort. It is therefore worth spending a little money and effort on draughtproofing your home.

Locating draughts
A lighted joss stick will detect the slightest draught.

Locating draughts

Tackle the exterior doors and windows first. Seal only those interior doors that are the worst offenders, as there should be some 'trickle' ventilation from room to room.

Next, check other possible sources of draughts – such as spaces between floorboards, gaps in skirtings, loft hatches, fireplace openings, and the overflow pipes from sanitaryware. Locate draughts by holding a lighted joss stick near likely gaps. You may be surprised by how much air is whistling through, especially on a windy day.

Draught excluders are made by a variety of manufacturers and there are many variations. Nevertheless, the following examples illustrate the principles that are commonly employed.

Threshold draught excluders

If the gap between the bottom of a door and the floor is very large, it's bound to admit fierce draughts, so it pays to use a threshold excluder to seal the gap.

If you fit an excluder to an exterior door, make sure it is suitably weatherproof. If you can't buy a threshold excluder that fits the opening exactly, cut a longer one down to size.

Flexible-strip excluders
The simplest form of threshold draught excluder is a flexible strip of plastic or rubber that sweeps against the floor-covering to form a seal. Most excluders have a rigid-plastic or aluminium extrusion that is screwed to the face of the door to hold the excluder in contact with the floor. Flexible-strip excluders work best over smooth flooring.

Brush seals
A long nylon-bristle brush, set into a metal or plastic extrusion, can be used to exclude draughts under doors. This kind of threshold excluder is suitable for slightly uneven floors and textured floorcoverings. It is the only type that can be fitted to sliding doors as well as hinged ones. Brush-depth varies a great deal, but provided the pile is in contact with the floor surface it should still work efficiently.

Flexible arch
This type of excluder consists of an arched vinyl insert, fitted to a shallow aluminium extrusion, that presses against the bottom edge of the door. Because it has to be nailed or screwed to the floor, a flexible-arch excluder is difficult to use on a solid-concrete floor. For an external door, choose a version that has additional underseals to prevent rain seeping beneath it. To fit it, you may have to plane the bottom edge of the door.

Door kits
The best solution for an exterior door is to buy a kit combining an aluminium weather trim, which is designed to shed rainwater, and a weather bar fitted with a tubular draught excluder that's made of rubber or plastic. The trim is screwed to the face of the door, and the weather bar is fixed to the threshold. There are a great many variations to choose from, but all work on a similar principle.

Screwing a weather trim to the door
Use a bradawl to mark the screw holes, especially on a hardwood door.

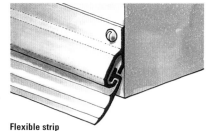

Flexible strip

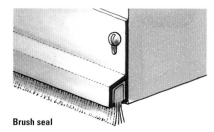

Brush seal

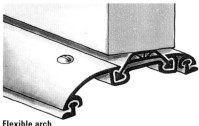

Flexible arch

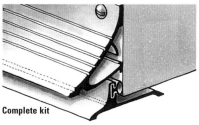

Complete kit

SEE ALSO > Grants 7

Sealing gaps around doors and casement windows

A well-fitting door needs a 2mm (1/16in) gap at the top and sides so that it can be operated smoothly. However, a gap this large can lose a great deal of heat. There are several ways to seal it, some of which are described here.

Hinged casement windows and pivot windows can be sealed with similar draught excluders, but check the excluders are weatherproof.

The cheaper excluders may have to be renewed regularly.

Compressible strips

The most straightforward excluder is a self-adhesive foam-plastic strip, which you stick around the rebate; the strip is compressed by the door or window, forming a seal. The cheapest polyurethane foam will be good for one or two seasons (although it's useless if painted) and is suitable for interior doors only. The better-quality vinyl-coated polyurethane, rubber or PVC foams are more durable and, unlike their cheaper counterparts, don't perish on exposure to sunlight. When applying compressible excluders, avoid stretching them, as that reduces their efficiency. The door or window may be difficult to close at first, but the excluder will adjust after a short while.

V-strips

If it is too difficult to force a door or casement closed against a compressible excluder, fit a strip that is bent back to form a V-shape. The self-adhesive strip can be mounted to fill the gap around the door or window, or attached to the stop so that the door or window closes against it. V-strips are cheap and unobtrusive, but a good fit is essential to exclude draughts completely.

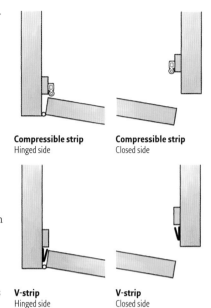

Compressible strip
Hinged side

Compressible strip
Closed side

V-strip
Hinged side

V-strip
Closed side

External-door sealer kits

1 Press strip against the door and insert screws

2 At each corner, cut a notch for a perfect fit

Foam strips are not suitable for external doors, although you can fit some of the rubber and plastic versions. Alternatively, buy an external-door sealer kit comprising three lengths of aluminium extrusion holding a plastic or rubber strip that presses against the outer face of the door across the top and down both sides. A flat strip is provided for fitting across the top and down the closing side. A curved strip is supplied for fitting to the doorframe down the hinged side. If you fit the strips to the wrong side of the door, the seal will be less effective.

Use a small hacksaw to cut each extrusion to size, taking an equal amount from each end. If the flexible strip gets wrinkled in the process, pinch one end of the extrusion onto the strip, using a pair of pliers. Pull on the other end of the strip to straighten it, and then pinch the extrusion at that end to keep the strip in tension.

With the door closed, hold the short extrusion against the top of the doorframe, with the flexible strip pressing against the door. Make sure the strip is pressed evenly across the door, then use a bradawl to mark the positions of the slotted fixing holes in the aluminium. Screw the extrusion in place (**1**). Make sure the strip seals properly across the door. If necessary, loosen the screws and adjust the position of the extrusion.

Repeat the process down both sides of the door, taking care to ensure the curved flexible strip on the hinged side does not get pinched by the edge of the door.

For a perfect seal, cut a notch out of both top corners to join the extrusions closely (**2**).

Keyholes and letter boxes

Keyhole coverplate
The coverplate is part of the escutcheon.

An external keyhole should be fitted with a coverplate to keep out draughts during the winter.

You can buy a hinged flap that screws onto the inside of the door to cover a letter box; some types have a brush seal behind the flap for extra draughtproofing.

Brush-seal excluder
An integral brush seal prevents draughts even when the letter box is open.

SEE ALSO > Grants 7, Draughtproofing sashes 20

Draughtproofing sashes

Draughtproofing the sliding components of a sash window is more complicated than sealing hinged casements. It's necessary to fit different types of excluder to the various parts of the window.

Sealing a sash window

The top and bottom closing rails of a sash window can be sealed with a weatherproof compressible excluder, but choose one that allows you to operate the latch when the sashes are closed.

The sliding edges admit fewer draughts, but they can be sealed with a brush seal fixed to the frame – inside for the lower sash, outside for the top one. With the brush pressed against the sash, drive panel pins through the predrilled holes into the framework.

To seal the gap between the sloping faces of the central meeting rails of a traditional sash window, use a self-adhesive springy V-strip.

Pin a brush seal to the staff bead

Replacing the beads

Professional companies that specialize in refurbishing sliding-sash windows can replace the parting beads and the inner staff beads with new ones that have integral brush seals. This will cost you a lot more than a DIY solution – but, in addition to superior draughtproofing, the refurbished windows will slide more smoothly and rattles will be eliminated.

Draughtproofed beads
Have a refurbishment company install beads made with integral brush seals.

Filling large gaps

Large gaps left around newly fitted window frames (or doorframes) will be a source of draughts. The same is true of a hole made for pipework or an air vent. Use an expanding-foam filler to seal these gaps. When the filler has set, trim off the excess and then seal around the frame with flexible mastic.

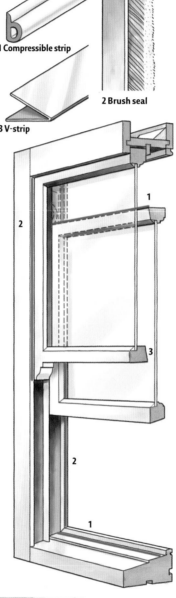

1 Compressible strip

2 Brush seal

3 V-strip

SEE ALSO > Grants 7, Draughtproofing doors and casements 19

Additional draughtproofing

The ventilated void below a suspended wooden floor is a common source of draughts that penetrate through large gaps between floorboards and under the skirting. Fill between floorboards or cover them with hardboard panels.

Seal gaps at the skirting boards with mastic applied with an applicator gun. Pin a quadrant or scotia moulding to the skirting to cover the sealed gap.

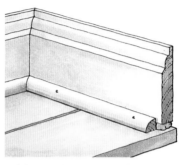

Seal the gap with mastic and wooden quadrant

Draughts from overflows

Overflow pipes leading directly from a lavatory cistern or cold-water storage tank frequently provide a passage for draughts when there's a strong wind blowing. This can cause pipes to freeze in harsh conditions.

The simplest solution is to cut the neck off a balloon and stretch it over the end of the pipe – the fabric will hang down to cover the opening but allow water to pass through unhindered.

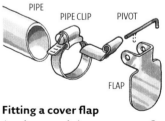

PIPE PIPE CLIP PIVOT FLAP

Fitting a cover flap

Another remedy is to cut a cover flap from a lightweight rustproof metal, such as zinc or aluminium. Make a simple pivot from the same metal and attach the flap to the end of the tube with a pipe clip.

Draughty fireplaces

To retain a disused open fireplace, cut a sheet of flame-retardant polystyrene to seal the throat of the chimney – leave a hole 50mm (2in) across for ventilation. If you use the fireplace again, don't forget to remove the polystyrene.

Insulating roofs

Approximately a quarter of the heat lost from an average house goes through the roof, so minimizing this should be one of your priorities. Provided you are able to gain access to your loft space, reducing heat loss through the roof is just a matter of laying insulating material between the joists – which is cheap, quick and effective. If you want to make use of your attic, insulating the sloping surface of the roof is a straightforward alternative.

Types of roof insulation

There's a range of insulating materials available, so investigate which type will suit your circumstances best.

Blanket insulation

Blanket insulation – which is made from glass fibre, mineral wool or rock fibre – is widely available in the form of rolls that fit snugly between the joists. All types are non-flammable and are proofed against damp and vermin. Similar material, cut to shorter lengths, is also sold as 'batts'.

Some blanket insulation is wrapped in plastic that serves as a vapour barrier (see below right) and reduces direct contact with fibres that could irritate the skin. However, unbacked blanket is the cheapest and it is perfectly suitable for laying on the loft floor.

Blankets are usually either 100, 150, 170 or 200mm (4, 6, 6¾ or 8in) thick. Some kinds can be split into two to accommodate shallow joists or for topping up existing insulation. The rolls are normally 370 to 400mm (15 to 16in) wide, to fit snugly between the joists, and 6 to 8m (20 to 25ft) long. Wider rolls are available for non-standard joist spacing.

If you want to fit blanket insulation to the sloping part of a roof, buy semi-rigid batts or slabs of mineral fibre, between 50 and 75mm (2 and 3in) thick. Similar materials can be inserted between the wall studs when insulating an attic.

Rigid sheet insulation

Sheet insulation, of foamed polystyrene or polyurethane, can be fixed between the rafters of a sloping roof. It pays to install the thickest insulation possible, allowing sufficient ventilation between the insulating material and the roof tiles or slates to avoid condensation.

Some polystyrene panels are grooved longitudinally, which makes them easy to cut to width, using a small craft saw. The grooves also allow the panels to be compressed slightly, which makes for a snug fit between the sloping rafters.

Foiled quilts

If the rafters are too narrow to accommodate slab or rigid sheet insulation, you could staple a thin foiled quilt to the underside of the roof timbers.

One type of quilt is made of layers of foamed plastic interleaved with reflective foil. This is relatively expensive, but the U-value of a layer 25mm (1in) thick is equivalent to that of standard blanket insulation eight times thicker.

Other quilts have a layer of superior-quality 'bubble wrap' sandwiched between foil. The same quilt is suitable for laying between the joists when insulating suspended wooden floors.

Rigid-foam decking

If you plan to use your loft for storage, consider laying foamed polystyrene panels with flooring-grade moisture-resistant chipboard bonded to the top surface. The edges of the chipboard are tongued and grooved for positive location. The panels, which are narrow enough to pass through most loft hatches, are laid at right angles to the joists. For a better standard of insulation, the panel manufacturers recommend laying blanket insulation between the joists before you lay the panels on top and screw them to the joists. You should provide sufficient gaps to allow heat to escape from ceiling-mounted uplighters and electrical cable.

Blown-fibre insulation

Inter-joist fibrous insulation is blown through a large hose by professional contractors. It may not be suitable for a house in a windy location, but seek the contractor's advice. An even depth of 270mm (10½in) is required to meet current recommendations. Discuss with the contractor how best to avoid burying electrical cables and light fittings under the insulation.

Preparing the loft

Before installing any form of insulation, check roof timbers for woodworm and signs of rot, so they can be treated first. Make sure all the electrical wiring is sound, and carefully lift it clear so that you can lay insulation beneath it. In some cases it may be necessary to install longer cables with sufficient slack to accommodate thicker insulation.

The plaster or plasterboard ceiling below will not support your weight. You therefore need to lay a plank or two, or a chipboard panel, across the joists so you can move about safely. If there is no permanent lighting in the loft, rig up an inspection lamp on an extension lead and move it wherever it is needed – or hang the lamp high up to provide an overall light.

Most attics are very dusty, so wear old clothes and a gauze face mask. It is also advisable to wear protective gloves, especially if you're handling glass-fibre batts or blanket insulation, which may irritate sensitive skin.

Vapour barriers

Installing roof insulation has the effect of making uninsulated parts of the house colder than before, so increasing the risk of condensation either on or within the structure itself. This could reduce the effectiveness of the insulation – and also promote dry rot in the roof timbers.

One way to prevent this happening is to ventilate those parts of the house that are outside the insulated area. Alternatively, install a vapour barrier on the warm (inner) side of the insulation, to prevent moisture-laden air passing through. The vapour barrier, which is usually a plastic or metal-foil sheet, is sometimes supplied along with the insulation. It's vital that the barrier is continuous and undamaged.

Some blankets are sleeved in plastic or foil and therefore do not require a separate vapour barrier. Other types of insulation have a closed-cell structure that resists the passage of water vapour – making it unnecessary to install a vapour barrier.

Working safely
Place strong planks or chipboard panels over the joists to make safe walkways in the loft.

Installing a vapour barrier
Cut the sheet into strips about 75mm (3in) wider than the joist spacing, then staple each strip to the joist on each side. Overlap any joints and secure with self-adhesive tape. Cut holes in the sheet to accommodate light fittings that protrude into the loft.

SEE ALSO > Ventilating the roof space 31

Insulating a loft

One of the easiest ways to insulate a loft that isn't in use as a living space is to lay blanket insulation between the joists. No special skills are required and the job should take no longer than a day to complete.

Laying blanket insulation

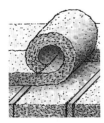

Cross-laying
Most modern ceiling joists are only 100mm (4in) deep. One way to install insulation of the recommended thickness is to lay two layers of blanket at right angles to each other.

Before starting to lay blanket insulation, seal gaps around pipes, vents or wiring entering the loft, using flexible mastic.

Remove the blanket's wrapping in the loft itself – the insulation is compressed for transportation and storage, but swells to its true thickness on being released – and begin by placing one end of a roll into the eaves. Make sure you don't cover the ventilation gap (trim the end of the blanket to a wedge shape, so that it doesn't obstruct the airflow), or fit eaves vents.

Unroll the blanket between the joists, pressing it down to form a snug fit – but don't compress it. Continue at the opposite side of the loft with another roll. Cut it to butt up against the end of the first roll, using either a large kitchen knife or a pair of long-bladed scissors. Continue across

the loft until all spaces have been filled (to fit odd spaces, trim the insulation).

Don't cover the casings of any light fittings that protrude into the loft space, and don't be tempted to cover electrical cables – there's a risk that they could over-heat. Instead, lay the cables on top of the blanket, taking care not to stretch them. If necessary, cut the blanket to leave a gap around and above a cable.

Don't insulate the area immediately below a cold-water tank – the heat rising from the room below will help to prevent freezing during the winter.

Cut a piece of blanket to fit the cover of the entrance hatch, and attach it with PVA adhesive or with cloth tapes and drawing pins. Fit foam draught excluder around the edges of the hatch.

Cross-laying insulation

The Building Regulations recommend a minimum thickness of 270mm (10½in) for loft insulation. Most ceiling joists are too shallow to accommodate blanket insulation of this thickness, and the only practical method of complying with the Regulations is to lay a second layer of insulation at right angles to the joists.

However, once the joists are covered it is impossible to walk in the loft without the danger of putting a foot through the plaster ceiling below. Even if you don't intend to use the loft for storage, you or a tradesman may have to enter the loft at some stage to service the plumbing or inspect the roof structure. Before laying a second layer of blanket insulation it makes sense to nail wooden spacers to the top of the joists in those areas where one may have to gain access, so you can place a chipboard flooring panel over the blanket and screw it down to the spacers. As you lay the blanket, cut it to fit around the spacers.

● **Ventilating the loft**
Laying insulation between the joists increases the risk of condensation in an unheated roof space – but provided there are adequate vents or gaps at the eaves, there will be enough air circulating to keep the loft dry.

Unwrap blanket insulation in the loft

Cut lengths to fit and butt them together

Laying blanket insulation
1 Gaps around pipes, vents and wiring are sealed.
2 Allowance for ventilation at the eaves.
3 Proprietary eaves vents keep the airway open permanently.
4 Blanket insulation laid between joists.
5 Tank and cold-water pipes insulated separately.

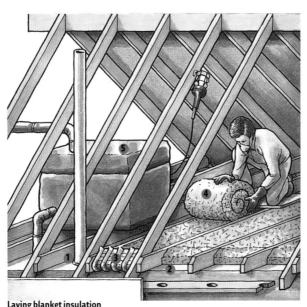
Laying blanket insulation

Tanks and pipes

Current bylaws require your cold-water-storage tank to be insulated. It's simplest to buy a Bylaw 30 kit, which includes a jacket and other equipment that is required. Insulate your central-heating expansion tank, too.

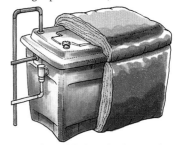
Buy a ready-made jacket to insulate a tank

Insulating pipes

If there are cold-water pipes running between the joists, prevent them from freezing by laying blanket insulation over them. If that's not practical, then insulate each pipe run separately, using foamed-plastic pipe lagging.

SEE ALSO > Lagging pipe runs 17, Draught excluders 19, Types of insulation 21, Ventilating the roof space 31

Insulating a sloping roof

If the attic is to be used as a room or rooms, you will need to insulate the sloping part of the roof in order to heat the living space. There's more than one solution to consider.

Insulating between the rafters

Repair the roof first, so the insulation won't become soaked in the event of leaks (it will also be more difficult to spot leaks after insulating).

Condensation often causes serious problems after installing insulation between the rafters, as the undersides of the roof tiles become very cold. It is vital to provide a 50mm (2in) gap between the insulant and the tiles, to promote sufficient ventilation to keep the space dry (this also determines the maximum thickness of insulation you can install). The ridge and eaves must be ventilated, and you should include a vapour barrier on the warm side of the insulation.

Attaching sheet insulation
Cut rigid sheet insulation as accurately as possible, to ensure a wedge-fit between the rafters. To maintain a 50mm (2in) gap behind the insulant, screw battens to the sides of the rafters (1); treat the new battens with a chemical preserver first.

Press the insulant in place, then staple a sheet of polythene vapour barrier over the rafters (2), making sure you double-fold the joints before stapling the polythene in place.

Lining with plasterboard.
Reduce heat loss still further by screwing insulated (thermal) plasterboard to the underside of the rafters. This is like ordinary plasterboard, but is backed up with a layer of insulating polystyrene. Insulated boards that have an integral vapour barrier do not require a separate plastic-sheet barrier. Screw the panels to the rafters, staggering the joints between.

Installing a foiled quilt

Where it is difficult to install adequate insulation between narrow rafters, you can staple a foiled quilt to the underside of the rafters.

Unroll the quilt as you work, cutting it to length with sharp scissors. Having stapled the quilt in place, seal the joints with a special foil tape that is made with an acrylic adhesive for a strong watertight bond.

If you want to plasterboard or panel over the quilt, screw spacer battens 25mm (1in) thick to the covered joists; then screw the boards to these battens. Use thermal plasterboard if the quilt alone does not provide sufficient insulation.

Using foiled quilt
Staple a foiled quilt to the underside of the rafters.

1 Screw battens to the sides of each rafter

2 Staple a vapour barrier over the rafters

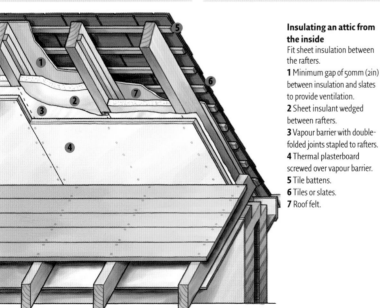

Insulating an attic from the inside
Fit sheet insulation between the rafters.
1 Minimum gap of 50mm (2in) between insulation and slates to provide ventilation.
2 Sheet insulant wedged between rafters.
3 Vapour barrier with double-folded joints stapled to rafters.
4 Thermal plasterboard screwed over vapour barrier.
5 Tile battens.
6 Tiles or slates.
7 Roof felt.

Insulating the attic

If there's an attic room that was built as part of the original structure of your house, you probably won't be able to insulate the pitch of the roof unless you are prepared to hack off the old plaster before insulating between the rafters (see left). It may therefore be simpler to insulate from the inside (as for a flat roof), although you won't have a great deal of headroom.

Insulate the short vertical wall of the attic from inside the crawlspace, installing a vapour barrier on the warm inner side of the partition. At the same time, insulate between the joists of the crawlspace.

Insulating a room in the attic
Surround the room itself with insulation – but leave the floor uninsulated, so the attic will benefit from heat rising from the rooms directly below.

Fit batts between the wall studs

SEE ALSO > Vapour barriers 21, Insulating flat roofs 24

Topping up

Most householders will have insulated the loft at some time in the past, but it is unlikely that existing insulation is thick enough to comply with the current recommendation of 270mm (10½in). You may wish to top up your present insulation to bring it up to standard.

Cross-laying

Laying a second layer of blanket insulation at right angles to the joists, which is described under insulating a loft, is a simple and effective way to reduce heat loss to a minimum.

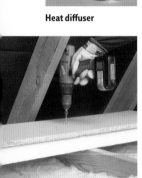

Heat diffuser

Rigid-foam decking

If you want to increase your insulation and, at the same time, convert your loft into a practical area for storage, you could install rigid-foam decking over your existing insulation. Make sure your ceiling joists are strong enough to take the additional load of insulation and any proposed storage.

If possible, maintain a gap between cables that are running over the existing insulation and the new foam decking in order to allow heat to dissipate. Alternatively, reroute cables over the decking. Cut the decking to allow access to light fittings that protrude into the loft space. A 75mm (3in) gap all round will be sufficient. You can buy proprietary heat diffusers that surround the light fittings to maintain a safe gap and prevent light fittings being dislodged accidentally as you move about the newly decked loft.

1 Screw to the joists

2 Glue the joints

Begin at the eaves, laying the first panels at right angles to the joists; secure each panel to the joists below with a single 150mm (6in) screw through the centre (**1**). Glue the tongued and grooved edges together to create a secure flat deck (**2**). Lay the next row, cutting the first panel in half in order to stagger the joints between the two rows.

As you lay subsequent panels, mark the position of pipe runs and cables on the surface of the decking for future reference. Cut the insulated panels to fit around cold-water storage tanks.

Rafter insulation

If electrical wiring or plumbing make installing extra insulation at joist level impracticable, leave the existing insulation in place and supplement it with foiled quilt or rigid sheet insulation fixed to the sloping roof above.

Insulating flat roofs

Expert contractors can insulate a flat roof from above, but the only practical DIY solution is to apply a layer of insulation to the ceiling.

Treatment from above

One way of insulating a flat roof is to lay rigid insulating board on the original deck. The bonded 'warm-roof system' incorporates a vapour barrier – possibly just the old covering – that is laid under the insulation, which is then protected with a new waterproof covering. With a protected-membrane system, the insulation is laid over the covering and is held in place with paving slabs or a layer of pebbles. Both systems are best installed by contractors. Get them to check that the roof is weatherproof and can support the additional weight.

Warm-roof system
(right)
1 Roof deck
2 Waterproof covering
3 New vapour barrier
4 Insulation
5 New waterproof covering

Protected-membrane system (far right)
1 Roof deck
2 Waterproof covering
3 Insulation
4 Paving slabs

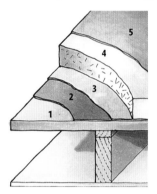

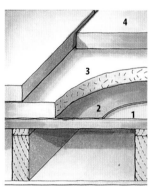

Treatment from below

Another option is to insulate the ceiling below a flat roof. This is not a difficult task, provided the area is not too large, but you will have to relocate lighting and accommodate windows or fitted cupboards that extend to the ceiling.

Very often the space within the roof structure has little or no ventilation. It is therefore essential to include a vapour barrier on the warm side of the ceiling, below the insulation.

First of all, either nail thermal plasterboard to the joists or install fire-retardant expanded polystyrene, 50mm (2in) thick, between softwood battens screwed to the joists every 400mm (1ft 4in) across the ceiling. Fit the first of the battens against the wall at right angles to the joists, then fit one at each end of the room. Butt the polystyrene against the first batten, then coat the back of it with polystyrene adhesive and fix it to the ceiling. Continue with alternate battens and panels until you reach the other side of the room, finishing with a batten against the wall.

Install a polythene vapour barrier, double-folding the joints and stapling them to convenient battens. Fix plasterboard panels to the battens with galvanized plasterboard nails. Stagger the joins between the panels, then fill the joins and finish ready for decorating as required.

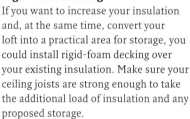

Insulating the ceiling
Insulate a flat roof by fixing insulant to the ceiling.
1 Existing plasterboard or lath-and-plaster ceiling.
2 Softwood battens screwed to the joists.
3 Insulation glued to existing ceiling.
4 Polythene vapour barrier stapled to the battens.
5 Plasterboard nailed to the battens.
6 If possible, provide cross-ventilation by installing vents equal to 0.4 per cent of the roof area.

SEE ALSO > Vapour barriers 21, Laying blanket insulation 22, Insulating a sloping roof 23, Thermal plasterboard 23

Insulating walls

Once you have recouped the initial outlay, insulating the external walls of your home will reduce your heating costs considerably.

Consider the options

How you insulate the walls of your home is likely to be determined by several factors. Firstly, the type of construction.

Cavity or solid walls

Houses built after 1920, and certainly after 1950, usually have cavity walls – two skins of masonry, with a gap between them to reduce the likelihood of water penetration. Although heat loss is slightly slower through a cavity wall than one of solid brick, that does not substantially reduce the cost of home heating. However, filling the cavity with insulation prevents circulation, trapping the air in millions of tiny air pockets within the material. This can reduce heat loss through the wall by as much as 65 per cent.

Solid walls require different treatment. You can either employ a contractor to insulate the external face of the walls or line the inner surfaces yourself.

Cavity insulation

Cavity filling is most cost-effective for homes that have properly controlled central heating. Heating without controls simply increases the temperature, instead of saving on fuel bills. This type of insulation is not practical for flats unless the whole building is insulated at the same time.

Dry-lining

Another method – suitable for solid and cavity walls – is to line the inner surfaces of the walls with insulation. This may involve a great deal of effort, depending on the amount of alteration to joinery, electrical fittings and plumbing required – but it does provide an opportunity for selective insulation, concentrating on those rooms that are likely to benefit most. It is also the only form of wall insulation that can be carried out by the householder.

Exterior-wall insulation

Cladding the exterior of a house with insulation is expensive and also spoils the appearance of most buildings. External-wall insulation can be installed only by a contractor and should only be considered if the house is built with solid masonry walls.

Insulating cavity walls

When constructing a new house, builders either include a layer of insulation between the two masonry leaves of exterior walls or blow insulant into the cavity before the walls are plastered on the inside. These measures significantly increase the insulation of the building. However, in the past, millions of homes were built with cavity walls that were left empty, and bringing these homes up to current standards of insulation requires a skilled professional to introduce an insulant through holes cut in the outer brick leaf.

Professional installers

It is imperative to hire contractors who specialize in blown cavity-wall insulation. Before starting work, the contractor will assess the house to ensure that the walls are suitable for filling, with no evidence of frost damage, failed pointing or cracked render. Leaking gutters will have to be repaired, too.

Having carried out the inspection, the contractor will complete and submit on your behalf a Building Notice to the local Building Control Office. When the work is complete, the contractor will ask the Cavity Insulation Guarantee Agency (CIGA) to issue a guarantee that covers the installation for 25 years against defects in workmanship or materials. The guarantee is transferable to future owners of the house. CIGA will honour the guarantee, even if the contractor goes out of business.

All systems of cavity-wall insulation have been tested and approved by independent bodies such as the British Board of Agrément (BBA). Amongst other requirements, the insulation must be water-resistant and must fill adequately in order to satisfy the BBA. The Board also undertake continuous assessment and surveillance of their approved installers.

Materials for blown cavity insulation

The most common type of cavity-wall insulation is mineral wool, being either rock wool or glass wool. One alternative to mineral wool is expanded polystyrene, (EPS), which comes in the form of white or grey beads. Along with the EPS, an adhesive is sprayed at the point of injection to bond the beads together and prevent the insulation settling in the cavity. EPS does not affect the fire resistance of the wall.

Urea-formaldehyde foam (UF) is rarely used except in the less exposed parts of the UK. Mineral wool and expanded polystyrene are approved for use all over the country.

Polyurethane-foam systems are generally used as cavity-reinforcement foam (CRF) where wall ties have corroded. CRF is considerably more expensive than other systems, and a CIGA guarantee is not available for it.

Installing the insulant

Any installation should be completed within 2 to 3 hours and is undertaken from outside the house, although the contractor will need to make various checks and tests inside. He or she will begin by drilling holes in a defined pattern through the mortar joints in the external walls (1). Extra holes are drilled close to obstructions such as doors and windows.

A hose is then inserted into each hole (2) and the insulant is blown into the cavity, filling it from the base. After injection, the holes are filled with mortar to match the existing pointing.

1 Drilling holes in the outer leaf

2 Introducing the insulant

SEE ALSO > Grants 7

Internal dry-lining

If you are planning to dry-line an external wall with some form of panelling, it is worth taking the opportunity to include blanket or sheet insulation between the wall-mounted furring strips.

Fix a polythene-sheet vapour barrier over the insulation by stapling it to the furring strips before you nail the panelling in place. Alternatively, use an insulated (thermal) plasterboard that has an integral vapour barrier.

Any form of panelling can be applied over blanket insulation, but you should use plasterboard to cover expanded-polystyrene insulant.

Insulated plasterboard
1 Insulant
2 Integral vapour barrier
3 Plasterboard lining

Gluing directly to the wall

A simpler method is to use the board manufacturer's adhesive to glue insulated plasterboard directly onto the wall. This type of wall insulation has a layer of plasterboard backed by a layer of either expanded-polystyrene or phenolic foam. Make sure an integral vapour barrier is incorporated into the board.

Using a trowel, apply 250 x 75mm (10 x 3in) dabs of adhesive to the wall, in three vertical rows, with a continuous strip of adhesive at the top and bottom. Place packing pieces of wood about 12 to 18mm (½ to ¾in) thick at the foot of the wall to support the insulated board.

Resting the bottom edge of the board on the packing pieces, press it against the adhesive and tamp it down with a 100 x 50mm (4 x 2in) straightedge. Apply each board in a similar way, making sure they are flat and level. Use a fine-toothed saw to cut a panel to fit into a corner.

For additional security, wait until the adhesive sets, then drill through each board into the wall to insert three nailable plugs, two near the top of the board and one in the centre. Remove the packing pieces, then tape and fill all joints.

Detailed instructions regarding door and window mouldings can be found in the section on wall panelling. Glue the skirting board to the plasterboard and seal the gap at the bottom with a bead of mastic sealant.

Gluing the plasterboard
Apply dabs of adhesive sealant to the wall in three rows.

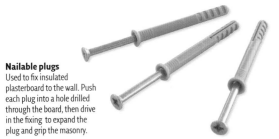

Nailable plugs
Used to fix insulated plasterboard to the wall. Push each plug into a hole drilled through the board, then drive in the fixing to expand the plug and grip the masonry.

Insulating floors

It is possible to upgrade an existing concrete floor by installing an insulated floating floor on top of it. You can reduce draughts through a suspended wooden floor, using carpet and underlay – but really effective insulation entails additional measures.

Working from above

By lifting the floorboards you can lay a substantial amount of insulation between the joists. Staple some plastic netting to the sides of the joists as support for blanket insulation. Alternatively, nail battens to the joists to support panels cut from rigid sheet insulant.

Installing foiled quilt

Another method is to roll foiled quilt across the floor joists and push it down between each pair of joists to a depth of 50mm (2in). Then staple the quilt to both sides of each joist. Overlap joints in the quilt by 100mm (4in) and take the insulation 75mm (3in) up behind the skirting boards.

Staple foiled quilt to the sides of the joists

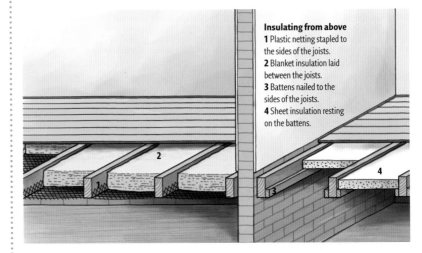

Insulating from above
1 Plastic netting stapled to the sides of the joists.
2 Blanket insulation laid between the joists.
3 Battens nailed to the sides of the joists.
4 Sheet insulation resting on the battens.

Working from below

If you can gain access from below, insulating a suspended wooden floor is easier still. Simply push insulating material between the joists and then staple plastic netting or wire mesh to the undersides to hold it in place.

Alternatively, run foiled quilt at right angles to the floor joists, stapling it to the undersides of the joists. Overlap the joints between strips of insulation by 100mm (4in).

Staple foiled quilt to the undersides of the joists

SEE ALSO > U-values 16, Types of roof insulation 21

Double glazing

A double-glazed window consists of two sheets of glass separated by an air gap. The air gap provides an insulating layer that reduces heat loss and sound transmission. Condensation is also reduced, because the inner layer of glass remains warmer than the glass on the outside.

Both factory-sealed units and secondary glazing are used for domestic double glazing. Sealed units are unobtrusive; secondary glazing is a cheaper option that helps to reduce the intrusion of noise from outside. Both provide good thermal insulation.

What size air gap?

For heat insulation, a 20mm (¾in) gap will give the optimum level of efficiency. If the gap is less than 12mm (½in), the air can conduct a proportion of the heat across it. If it's greater than 20mm (¾in), there is no appreciable gain in thermal insulation, and air currents can transmit heat to the outside layer of glass.

For noise insulation, an air gap of 100 to 200mm (4 to 8in) is more effective. Triple glazing – a combination of sealed units with secondary glazing – may therefore prove to be the ideal solution.

Although the amount of heat lost through windows is relatively small, the installation of double glazing can halve the wastage. As a result, you will find there is a saving on your fuel bills.

But the benefit you will be aware of more immediately is the elimination of draughts. In addition, the cold spots associated with large windows (most noticeable when you're sitting still) are likely to be reduced.

Installing double glazing with good window locks will improve security against forced entry, particularly when sealed units or toughened glass are used. However, make sure that some accessible part of appropriate windows can be opened in order to provide an escape route in case of fire.

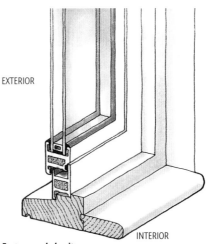

EXTERIOR

INTERIOR

Factory-sealed unit
A complete frame system installed by a contractor.

Double-glazed sealed unit

Heat-retentive sealed unit

AIR GAP

LOW-EMISSIVITY GLASS

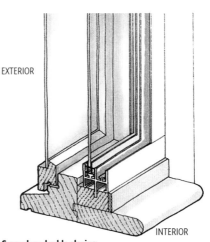

EXTERIOR

INTERIOR

Secondary double glazing
Fitted in addition to an ordinary glazed window.

Double-glazed sealed units

Double-glazed sealed units consist of two panes of glass that are separated by a spacer and hermetically sealed all round. The gap may contain dehydrated air – which eliminates condensation between the two panes of glass – or inert gases, which also improve thermal and acoustic insulation.

The thickness and type of glass used are determined by the size of the unit. Clear float glass or toughened glass is commonly employed. When obscured glazing is required to provide privacy, patterned glass is used. Heat-retentive sealed units, incorporating special low-emissivity glass, are supplied by some double-glazing companies.

Generally, factory-sealed units are produced and installed by suppliers of ready-made double-glazed replacement windows. Square-edged units are available for frames with a deep rebate, and stepped units for window frames that were originally intended for single glazing.

Double-glazed sealed units with metal-reinforced uPVC frames are rarely suitable for older houses. A secondary system that leaves the original window intact is generally more appropriate – especially if you have attractive leaded windows, which should be preserved (sealed units with a modern interpretation of leaded lights are not an adequate substitute for the real thing).

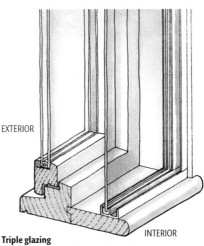

EXTERIOR

INTERIOR

Triple glazing
A combination of secondary and sealed units.

SEE ALSO > Secondary double glazing 28, Hinged and sliding systems 29

Secondary double glazing

Secondary double glazing consists of a separate pane of glass or plastic fitted over an ordinary single-glazed window. It is normally fitted on the inside of the existing windows, and is one of the most popular methods of double glazing as it's relatively inexpensive compared with sealed units. You can install DIY secondary-glazing kits yourself or stretch plastic film over your existing windows.

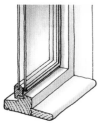

Sash-fixed
Glazing fixed to opening part of window.

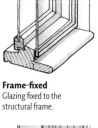

Frame-fixed
Glazing fixed to the structural frame.

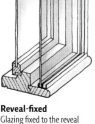

Reveal-fixed
Glazing fixed to the reveal and interior windowsill.

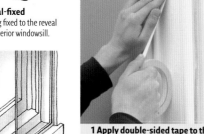

Exterior-fitted
Glazing fixed to the reveal and exterior windowsill..

● **Providing a fire escape**
If you fit secondary glazing, make sure there is at least one window in every occupied room that can be opened easily.

How double glazing is fixed

Secondary glazing can be fastened to the sash frames or window frame or across the window reveal. The method depends on ease of fixing, the type of glazing chosen, and the amount of ventilation that is required.

Glazing fixed to the sash will reduce heat loss through the glass and provide accessible ventilation – but it won't stop draughts, whereas glazing fixed to the window frame has the advantage of cutting down heat loss and eliminating draughts at the same time. Glazing fixed across the reveal offers improved noise insulation too, since the air gap can be wider. Any system should be readily demountable, or preferably openable, to provide a change of air if the room does not have any other form of ventilation.

A rigid-plastic or glass pane can be fitted to the exterior of the window if secondary glazing fitted on the inside would look unsightly. Windows set in a deep reveal, such as the sliding-sash type, are generally the most suitable ones for external secondary glazing.

Glazing with renewable film

Cheap and effective double glazing can be achieved using double-sided adhesive tape to stretch a thin flexible sheet of plastic across a window frame. The taped sheet can be removed and thrown away at the end of the winter.

Clean the window frame and cut the plastic roughly to size, allowing an overlap all round. Apply double-sided tape to the edges of the frame (**1**), then peel off the backing paper.

Attach the plastic film to the top rail (**2**), then tension it onto the tape on the sides and bottom of the window frame. Apply light pressure until you have positioned the film, and then rub it down onto the tape.

Remove all wrinkles in the film, using a hairdryer set to a high temperature (**3**). Starting at an upper corner, move the dryer slowly across the film, holding it about 6mm (¼in) from the surface. When the film is taut, cut off excess plastic with a knife (**4**).

1 Apply double-sided tape to the fixed frame

2 Stretch the film across the top of the frame

3 Use a hairdryer to shrink the film

4 Trim the waste with a sharp knife

Demountable systems

Other simple methods of interior secondary glazing use clear-plastic film or sheet. These lightweight materials are held in place by self-adhesive strips or rigid moulded sections, which form a seal. Most strip fastenings use magnetism or some form of retentive tape, thus allowing the secondary glazing to be removed for cleaning or ventilation. The strips and tapes usually have a flexible-foam backing, which takes up slight irregularities in the woodwork. You need to clean the windows and the surfaces of the window frame before installation. This type of secondary glazing can be left in place throughout the winter and removed for storage during the summer months.

Fitting demountable systems
To install the simplest systems, cut the plastic sheet to size, then hold it against the window frame and draw round it. Lay the sheet on a flat table. Peel back the protective paper from one end of the self-adhesive strip and stick it to the plastic sheet, flush with one edge. Cut the strip to length and repeat on the other edges. Cut the mating parts of the strips and stick them onto the window frame, following the guide lines marked earlier. Press the glazing into place.

When using rigid moulded sections, cut the sections to length with mitred corners. To fit an extruded clip-type moulding, stick the base section to the frame, then insert the outer section to hold the glazing in place.

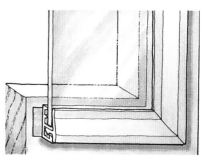

Rigid plastic mouldings support the glazing

SEE ALSO > Draughtproofing windows 20

Hinged and sliding systems

The suppliers of hinged or sliding secondary-glazing kits provide detailed fitting instructions for every situation. The description below will give you some idea of the work involved and, if you prefer, you can ask the same companies to install similar systems for you. Sliding and hinged systems are intended to be permanent fixtures.

Glass or plastic

Self-assembly kits can incorporate glass of various thicknesses to suit the location, but if your window is close to the floor, or is vulnerable to impact damage for some other reason, you may prefer to use clear acrylic sheet instead.

Hinged systems

Hinged systems incorporate coated aluminium extrusions that form a frame for the glass or rigid-plastic sheet. The glazing sits in a flexible gasket lining the extrusions. Screw-fixed corner joints hold the sides of the frame together, and pivot hinges are inserted into one of the extrusions in order to make side-hung or top-hung units.

Hinged units are usually fitted to the face of a wooden window frame and secured by turn buttons. A flexible draughtproofing strip is fixed to the back of the frame. A self-locking stay can be fitted to keep the window open to provide ventilation.

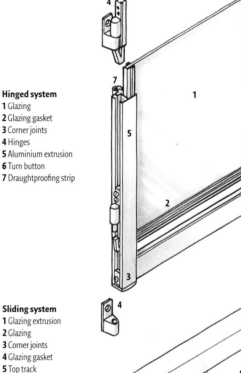

Hinged system
1 Glazing
2 Glazing gasket
3 Corner joints
4 Hinges
5 Aluminium extrusion
6 Turn button
7 Draughtproofing strip

Sliding systems

A horizontally sliding system is used for casement windows, whereas a vertically sliding system is more suitable for tall double-hung sashes. Each of the panes is framed by an aluminium extrusion, which is jointed at the corners, and the glass is sealed into its frame with a gasket.

A horizontal system has two or more sliding panes, the number depending on the width of the window. They are held in a tracked frame, which is screwed to the window frame or to the reveal. Fibre or brush seals are fitted to the sliding-frame members to prevent draughts. The glazing is opened with an integral handle, and each pane can be lifted out for cleaning.

A vertically sliding system is similar in construction, but catches are incorporated to hold the panes open at any height.

Fitting a horizontally sliding system
As an example of what is involved, the following instructions describe the installation of a sliding system often used for casement windows. Suppliers provide more detailed instructions with their kits.

Measure your window opening and buy a kit of parts slightly larger than the opening. After cutting the vertical track members to size, using a hacksaw (1), screw them to either the reveal or the inside face of the window frame. Cut the top and bottom track members and screw them in place (2) after cutting notches in the extrusions to fit the shape of the side members (see right). This frame must be square and parallel if the glazed frames are to slide smoothly.

Measure the opening for the glazing and have it cut to size, following manufacturer's instructions regarding tolerances. Cut and fit the components of the glazing frames, including gaskets and seals. Join the four sides together with corner joints (3) – and lift the glazing into the sliding tracks (4).

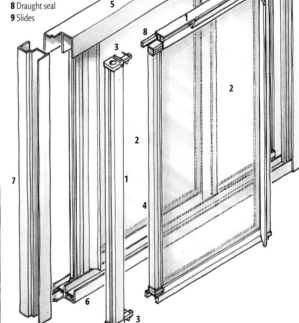

Sliding system
1 Glazing extrusion
2 Glazing
3 Corner joints
4 Glazing gasket
5 Top track
6 Bottom track
7 Side track
8 Draught seal
9 Slides

1 Cut track to length

2 Screw it in place

3 Assemble the frame

4 Fit it into the tracks

SEE ALSO > Double glazing 27

Heat-recovery ventilation

It has been estimated that more than half the energy produced by burning fossil fuels is used simply to keep our homes warm. Although the installation of efficient insulation reduces heat loss to a minimum, a great deal of heat is still wasted as a result of necessary ventilation.

Heat-recovery ventilators

Heat-recovery ventilators are designed to balance the requirements of conserving energy and the need for a constant supply of clean fresh air. But in practice the cost of running the system may outweigh the benefits of heat recovery.

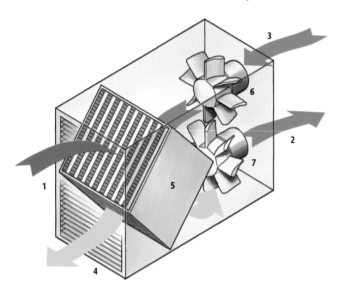

Heat-recovery ventilation unit
The diagram shows the layout of a typical wall-mounted heat-recovery ventilator.
1 Stale air from room
2 Stale-air exhaust
3 Fresh-air supply
4 Warmed fresh air
5 Heat exchanger
6 Induction fan
7 Extractor fan

How it works

Heat-recovery ventilation can range in scale from compact airbrick-size units, for continuous low-volume ventilation of individual rooms, to whole-house ducted systems. The simple ventilator shown below left contains two low-noise electric fans. Stale air from the interior is extracted by one fan through a highly efficient heat exchanger. This absorbs up to 70 per cent of the heat that would otherwise be wasted, and transfers it to a flow of fresh air drawn into the room by the second fan. Because the two airflows are not allowed to mingle, odours and water vapour are not transferred along with the heat.

Dehumidifiers control condensation

To combat condensation, you can either remove the moisture-laden air by ventilation or warm it so that it is able to carry more water vapour before it becomes saturated. A third possibility is to extract the water itself from the air, using a dehumidifier.

A dehumidifier works by drawing air from the room into the unit and passing it over a set of cold coils, so that the water vapour condenses on them and drips into a reservoir. The cold but now dry air is then drawn by a fan over heated coils before being returned to the room as additional convected heat.

The process is based on the simple refrigeration principle that gas under pressure heats up – and when the pressure drops, the temperature of the gas drops too. In a dehumidifier, a compressor delivers pressurized gas to the 'hot' coils, in turn leading to the larger 'cold' coils, which allow the gas to expand. The cooled gas then returns to the compressor for recycling.

A dehumidifier for domestic use is usually built into a floor-standing cabinet. It contains a humidistat that automatically switches on the unit when the moisture content of the air reaches a predetermined level. When the reservoir is full, the unit shuts down in order to prevent overflowing, and an indicator lights up to remind you to empty the water in the container.

Fitting a heat-recovery ventilator

Site a heat-recovery ventilator on an external wall, close to the ceiling and in a position where it will extract air most efficiently. Although they are typically set into a standard solid or cavity wall, you can install one in a thicker wall with the aid of a telescopic metal sleeve.

After marking out the aperture, cut away the masonry. Fit the unit into the hole and repair the masonry and plasterwork, sealing any gaps around the unit with a gun-applied sealant. Finally, wire up the controls of the ventilator, following the manufacturer's instructions.

When a dehumidifier is installed in a damp room, it should extract the excess moisture from the furnishings and fabric within a week or two. After that, it will monitor the moisture content of the air to maintain a stabilized atmosphere.

Working components of a dehumidifier

1 Incoming damp air	**6** Fan
2 Cold coils	**7** Dry warm air
3 Water reservoir	**8** Capillary tube where gas
4 Compressor	expands
5 Hot coils	

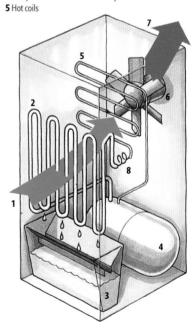

Air-conditioning units

With increasing summer temperatures to contend with, people are looking for a simple means of installing air conditioning, even if only for one or two rooms. One solution is to fit a compact wall-mounted unit that can cool, warm or dehumidify the air at the press of a button on its remote controller.

The refrigerant system in this type of unit is factory-sealed, so installation does not involve having to connect pipes or hoses. All that is required are two 155mm (6in) holes bored at a slight downward angle through an external wall. Outside, there's no unsightly condensing unit but simply a pair of discreet grilles.

The unit is powered by electricity from a fused connection unit mounted inside the room.

Ventilating the roof space

When loft insulation first became popular as an energy-saving measure, householders were recommended to tuck insulant right into the eaves to keep out draughts. What people failed to recognize was that a free flow of air is necessary in the roof space to prevent moisture-laden air from below condensing on the structure.

Inadequate ventilation can lead to serious deterioration. Wet rot develops in the roof timbers and water drips onto the insulant, eventually rendering it ineffective as insulation. If water builds up into pools, the ceiling below becomes stained and there is a risk of short-circuiting the electrical wiring in the loft. For these reasons, efficient ventilation of the roof space is essential in every home.

Ventilating the eaves

The regulations governing new housing insist on ventilation equivalent to continuous openings of 10mm (3/8in) along two opposite sides of a roof that has a pitch (slope) of 15 degrees or more. If the pitch is less than 15 degrees or the roof space is habitable, ventilation must be equivalent to continuous openings of 25mm (1in). It makes sense to adopt similar standards when refurbishing a house of any age. The simplest method of ventilating a standard pitched roof is to fit soffit vents made with integral insect screens. To calculate how many vents you need, divide the specified airflow capacity of the vent you are planning to use into the recommended continuous gap. Space the vents evenly along the roof. Push the vents into openings cut with a hole saw or jigsaw.

If the opening at the eaves is likely to be restricted by insulation, insert a plastic or cardboard eaves vent between each pair of joists. Push the vent into the angle between the rafters and the joists, with the ribbed section uppermost. Vents can be cut to length with scissors for an exact fit. When you install the insulation, push it up against the vent.

Slate and tile vents

Certain types of roof construction do not lend themselves to ventilation from the eaves only, but the structure can be ventilated successfully by strategically replacing tiles or slates with specially designed roof vents. A range of colours and shapes is available to blend with various roof coverings.

Venting the roof

Eaves-to-eaves ventilation normally keeps the roof space dry, but tile or slate vents sometimes have to be fitted to draw air through the roof space.

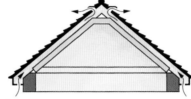

An attic space
If you insulate a sloping roof, you must provide a minimum 50mm (2in) airway between the insulant and roof covering. Fit soffit vents at the eaves, and replace some tiles or slates near the ridge with vents.

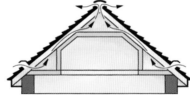

A room in the roof
Where a room is built into the attic, fit ridge vents and tile or slate vents near the eaves to draw air through the narrow spaces over the sloping ceiling.

A fire wall or party wall
Fit slate or tile vents to ventilate your side of the wall (ideally, your neighbour should do the same). Use a similar arrangement to ventilate a mono-pitch roof over an extension or lean-to.

A flat roof
An insulated flat roof can be ventilated by fitting over-fascia ventilators at the eaves and at the wall abutment. On an existing roof, you need to modify the wall flashing.

Soffit vent

Slate/tile vents
Roof vents are made to resemble a variety of roof coverings.

Ridge vent

Slate vent

Double pantile vent

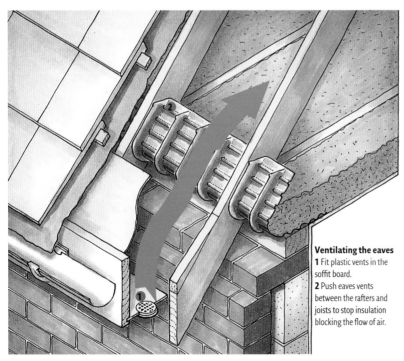

Ventilating the eaves
1 Fit plastic vents in the soffit board.
2 Push eaves vents between the rafters and joists to stop insulation blocking the flow of air.

SEE ALSO > Insulating a loft 21–4, Insulating a sloping roof 23

Whole-house ventilation

If you are prepared to make the necessary investment, you can have a simple system installed to extract moisture-laden air and stale odours from the entire house. It works on the principle that natural convection draws the relatively warm air inside the house via ducts to the roof, where it escapes through ridge or tile vents. This type of system is self-regulating and, since there are no electrical connections, it costs absolutely nothing to run.

Passive stack ventilation

Extractors are fitted in rooms where there is likely to be the greatest concentration of moist or odour-laden air – usually the kitchen, bathroom and utility room. A single duct runs from each extractor by the most direct route to the roof, where the wind creates a suction effect that helps to draw the warm air through the duct, just like smoke being carried up a chimney. The stale air in neighbouring 'dry' rooms, such as living rooms and bedrooms, moves naturally towards the vented rooms where extraction takes place. Trickle vents, fitted in the windows or exterior walls of the dry rooms, provide a flow of fresh air.

● **Noise pollution**
Because there are no fans running, passive stack ventilation is perfectly quiet. If there is a possibility of noise penetrating from outside, make sure the air-inlet vents are fitted with acoustic baffles.

Ventilation by demand
The inlet vents and extractors in each room are operated by humidity-sensitive controls, so that their flaps or louvres open and close progressively to admit or extract air as necessary, to maintain a perfect balance.

Unobtrusive installation
Provided that they are fitted with care, the system's slim external vents should be unobtrusive. Internally, ducting is normally either sited within fitted cupboards or run through stud partitions up to the roof space, where it must be insulated to prevent condensation forming inside the duct.

● **Combustion air**
Rooms containing open-flued heating appliances must be ventilated permanently. Suitable vents can be installed as part of passive-vent systems.

Extracting radon

Radon is a radioactive gas that can seep into buildings from below ground. Mostly, radon levels are so low they are harmless, but where the gas is sufficiently concentrated it can be a health risk. When building new homes, contractors must prevent radon gas from entering the building. This is done by incorporating a gas-impermeable membrane in a solid concrete base. Below a suspended floor, ventilation is usually sufficient to disperse the gas. Where there are high concentrations, install a radon-collection sump below ground, vented to the roof.

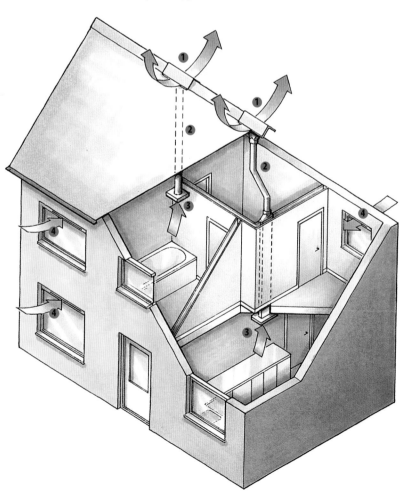

● **Passive-vent system**
This type of system is designed to ventilate the entire house without using electrically driven fans.
1 Stale moist air escapes through ridge vents (as shown) or through tile vents, which must be located no more then 50cm (20in) from the ridge.
2 Ducting takes the shortest route to the roof. Air is drawn through the vents by convection.
3 Extractors in the kitchen and bathroom draw air from surrounding rooms.
4 Trickle vents mounted in windows or exterior walls admit fresh air but without causing draughts.

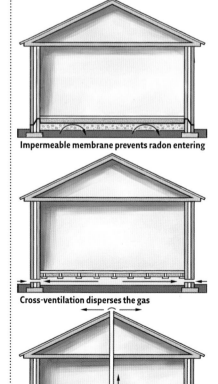

Impermeable membrane prevents radon entering

Cross-ventilation disperses the gas

A vented sump removes radon by convection

SEE ALSO > Central-heating boilers 58

Conserving power and water

Simple changes in habit – such as remembering to switch off unnecessary lighting and leaving the lawn sprinkler in the garden shed – can make a difference to your consumption of electrical power and mains water, but there are more far-reaching initiatives that could reduce your electricity and water bills still further.

Are you buying your electricity and gas from the cheapest source? Prices fluctuate so regularly that it can be difficult to keep up, but there are websites you can visit that will help you decide whether it is worth switching to another supplier.

Maintaining your plumbing system should help prevent water from leaking away and you can fit special taps and shower sprayheads that consume less water. Better still, why not collect rainwater in a water butt beside the house? This will provide you with adequate water for the garden next time there's a hosepipe ban. If you want to invest a larger sum of money in water conservation, you could install an underground storage tank from which you can draw off water for flushing your WCs and washing your laundry.

Many people would like to switch to alternative energy sources, such as wind power or solar energy. If you are building a new home from scratch you have a much wider range of options at your disposal, but at the very least you can install solar collectors that will reduce the amount of electricity you need to heat your water.

Reducing electricity bills

Pressures from all sides urge us to conserve energy. But even without such encouragement, our electricity bills would provide stimulus enough to make us find ways of using less power. Nobody wants to live in a poorly heated or dismally lit house without the comforts of hot water, refrigeration and other conveniences – but it is possible to identify where energy is wasted and find ways to reduce waste without compromising comfort or pleasure.

Fitting controls to save money

As the chart opposite clearly shows, heating is by far the biggest consumer of domestic power. One way to reduce your electricity bills is to fit devices that regulate the heating in your home to suit your lifestyle, maintaining comfortable but economic temperatures.

Thermostats

Most modern heating has some form of thermostatic control – a device that will switch power off when surroundings reach a certain temperature. Many thermostats are marked out simply to increase or decrease the temperature, in which case you have to experiment with various settings to find the one that suits you best. If the thermostat settings are more precise, try 18°C (65°F) for everyday use – although elderly people are more comfortable at about 21°C (70°F).

As well as saving you money, an immersion-heater thermostat prevents your water from becoming dangerously hot. Set it at 60°C (140°F). See right for Economy 7 settings.

Time switches

Even when it's thermostatically controlled, heating is expensive if run continuously – but you can install an automatic time switch to turn it on and off at preset times, so you get up in the morning and arrive home in the evening to a warm house. Set it to turn off the heating about half an hour before you leave home or go to bed, as the house will take time to cool down.

A similar device will ensure that your water is at its hottest when needed.

● **Insulation**
Measures taken to save energy will have little effect unless you insulate your house as well as the hot-water cylinder and pipework. You can do most of the work yourself for a relatively modest outlay and a little effort.

Off-peak rates

Electricity is normally sold at a general-purpose rate, every unit used costing the same; but if you warm your home with storage heaters and heat your water electrically, then you can take advantage of the economical off-peak tariff. This system, called Economy 7, allows you to charge storage heaters and heat water at less than half the general-purpose rate for seven hours, starting between midnight and 1 a.m. Other appliances used during that time get cheap power too, so more savings can be made by running the dishwasher or washing machine after you've gone to bed. Each appliance must, of course, be fitted with a timer. The Economy 7 daytime rate is higher than the general-purpose one, but the cost of running 24-hour appliances such as freezers and refrigerators is balanced since they also use cheap power for seven hours.

For full benefit from off-peak water heating, use a cylinder that holds 182 to 227 litres (40 to 50 gallons), to store as much cheap hot water as possible. You will need a twin-element heater or two separate units. One heater, near the base of the cylinder, heats the whole tank on cheap power; another, about half way up, tops up the hot water during the day. Set the night-time heater at 75°C (167°F), the daytime one at 60°C (140°F).

The electricity companies provide Economy 7 customers with a special meter to record daytime and night-time consumption separately, plus a timer that automatically switches the supply from one rate to the other.

Monitoring consumption

Keep an accurate record of your energy saving by taking weekly readings. Note the dates of any measures taken to cut power consumption, and compare the corresponding drop in meter readings.

Digital meters

Modern meters display a row of digits that represent the total number of units consumed since the meter was installed. To calculate the number of units used since your last electricity bill, simply subtract the 'present reading' shown on your bill from the number of units now shown on the meter. Make sure that the bill gives an actual reading and not an estimate (indicated by the letter 'E' before the reading).

Reading dial meters

Older installations may incorporate a meter with a set of dials that indicate the consumption of electricity. With a bit of practice you will be able to read these meters yourself. Ignore the dial marked ¹⁄₁₀, which is only for testing. Start with the dial indicating single units (kWh) and, working from right to left, record the readings from the 10, 100, 1000 and finally 10,000 unit dials. Note the digits the pointers have passed. If a pointer is, say, between 5 and 6, record 5. If it's right on a number, say 8, check the next dial on the right: if that pointer is between 9 and 0, record 7; if it's past 0, record 8. Also, remember that adjacent dials revolve in opposite directions, alternating along the row.

Digital meter display

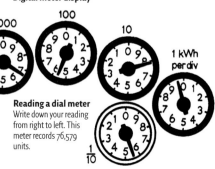

Reading a dial meter
Write down your reading from right to left. This meter records 76,579 units.

SEE ALSO > Insulation 16–29, Heating controls 61

Lower running costs

In Britain there are now more than twenty companies who supply electricity and gas – which means that shopping around may help you find a better deal. Supply companies play no part in the actual generation and distribution of electricity and gas, even if their parent company is involved with these activities. Whichever supplier you go with, the responsibility for meters and incoming cables and pipes remains unchanged.

Buying your energy at the lowest price

The tariffs offered by all the energy-supply companies are a combination of a standing charge and unit costs for the energy supplied. Unit costs vary, depending on whether the energy is supplied during the day or at night, and block charges for consumption above a certain level may reduce unit costs still further. In addition, discounts are usually available if you adopt methods of payment such as direct debit that are more convenient for the supply companies. There is also some incentive to choose a company who can supply both electricity and gas. Every company seeks to make its tariffs seem more attractive than those of its competitors – but the only figure that is important to you, the customer, is the total you pay each year for your energy.

Comparing prices
The government website **www.energywatch.org.uk** provides a code to be followed by price-comparison websites. Examples of websites that adhere to this code are **www.energylinx.co.uk**, **www.which.co.uk** and **www.uSwitch.com**
These sites will supply you with estimates of costs from each supplier and compare those against your present outgoings. Make sure you don't log on to a website created on behalf of one particular supplier. Once

you have made the choice to switch to another supplier, it is often possible to make the transfer on-line.

You can use the same 'comparison' sites to check on how easy it is to make a transfer to a potential supplier and find out what policies they have in relation to environmentally sensitive issues.

To carry out a meaningful comparison you will need to supply:
• Your postcode
• Your present suppliers of gas and electricity
• The type of meter (normal or Economy 7)
• Your annual consumption of each fuel or your present annual bills.
• The units used at night (for Economy 7 customers) expressed as either a number of units or a percentage of the total units

Though most companies offer discounts for customers who take both gas and electricity from the same supplier, you may find that it is more economical to purchase each fuel separately. Try entering the same details for gas and electricity only and compare the results with a quote for a combined tariff.

Within the constraints imposed by the government watchdog, energy suppliers are continually adjusting their prices, and it may be worth comparing costs at about the same time each year.

Energy-efficiency labelling

When you're shopping for new appliances, look for the European Community Energy Label that must by law be available at the point of sale, including web sites on the internet. This labelling gives guidance on energy efficiency for electrical equipment from light bulbs to dishwashers, and the choice of an 'A' rating can make considerable savings in running costs.

European flower
Any appliance bearing this symbol will be the best in its class in terms of all environmental criteria.

Energy
Manufacturer
Model

Fridge-Freezer ——— Type of appliance

More efficient
A ◄ **A** — This appliance is rated among the best for energy conservation.
B
C
D
E
F
G
Less efficient

Energy consumption kWh/year **325** — Under test conditions, the energy consumption of this appliance per year is 325kWh.
(Based on standard test results for 24h)

Actual consumption will depend on how the appliance is used and where it is located

Fresh food volume l   190 — Additional information – in this case the capacity of the fridge and freezer compartments.
Frozen food volume l   126

Noise
(dB(A) re 1 pW)

Further information is contained in product brochures — Noise level when running – not relevant for this appliance.

Norm EN 153 May 1990
Refrigerator Label Directive 94/2/EC

Typical running costs

Apart from the standing charge, your electricity bill is based on the number of units of electricity you have consumed during a given period. Each unit represents the amount used in one hour by a 1kW appliance. An appliance rated at 3kW will use the same amount of energy in 20 minutes. To help you identify the heavy users of energy, the chart on the right groups typical appliances under headings for low, medium and high electricity consumption.

LOW ENERGY CONSUMERS Less than 100 units per year	MEDIUM ENERGY CONSUMERS 100 to 1000 units per year	HIGH ENERGY CONSUMERS More than 1000 units per year
Toasters	Refrigerators	Instant water heaters
Coffee percolators	Freezers	Dishwashers
Slow cookers	Cookers	Immersion water heaters
Cooker hoods	Electric kettles	Fan heaters
Microwave ovens	Extractor fans	Electric fires
VCRs and DVD players	Washing machines	Whole-house lighting using GLS lamps (ordinary bulbs)
Stereo systems	Tumble dryers	Whole-house electric heating
Electric blankets	Irons	
Shavers	Vacuum cleaners	
Hairdryers	Colour TVs	
Power tools	Compact fluorescent house lighting	
Hedge trimmers	Instant showers	
Lawn mowers	Heated towel rails	

SEE ALSO ▷ Heating water 52–4, Comparing bulbs and tubes 37

Lamps and lighting

After heating, lighting tends to contribute most to domestic electricity bills. Our current levels of sophisticated and stylish illumination require a great many individual lamps (light bulbs) or fluorescent tubes. One government objective is to persuade householders to replace their conventional lamps with compact fluorescent tubes, which are far more energy-efficient. However, each type has its advantages and disadvantages, and some work better in certain locations than others.

Light bulbs and tubes

Although there are plans to outlaw the use of anything but low-energy lamps, at the present time there are numerous bulbs and tubes to choose from.

General lighting service lamps (GLS)
This is the trade name for what we call a light bulb. It is technically known as a tungsten-filament lamp, as the thin metal filament inside the glass envelope glows brightly when heated by electricity.

GLS bulbs come with either an Edison screw or a bayonet fitting for securing the bulb in a lampholder.

The glass envelope can be clear, for fitting inside or behind a glass or plastic cover; or 'pearl', which provides a diffused light for pendant fittings and table lamps. There are also coloured GLS lamps, used mainly for outdoor decorations.

As well as the familiar domed and compact mushroom-shaped bulbs, there are decorative GLS lamps, including bulbs shaped to resemble candle flames.

Tungsten-filament lamps create more heat than light, which is why they are relatively inefficient.

Reflector lamps
Some tungsten-filament lamps are silvered to reflect the light forwards or backwards.

Halogen lamps
The filament inside a bulb containing halogen gas glows with an intense white light. As well as mains-voltage lamps, there are low-voltage fittings that have to be wired to a transformer. However, low-voltage does not necessarily mean low-energy.

Halogen lamps are extremely popular for their bright 'sparkling' illumination, and are often found in miniature ceiling lights.

Double-ended halogen lamps are used in some outdoor light fittings. Provided it does not compromise your security, you could substitute lamps with a lower wattage to save electricity.

Fluorescent tubes
A fluorescent glass tube contains mercury vapour. The voltage makes electrons flow between the electrodes at the ends of the tube and bombard an internal coating – which fluoresces, producing bright light. Different types of coating make the light appear 'warmer' or 'cooler'. For domestic purposes, choose either 'warm white' or 'daylight' tubes.

The larger fluorescent light fittings are unattractive in most domestic interiors, but they are very functional for garages and workshops, where good even illumination is an advantage. They also provide practical worktop lighting when installed beneath kitchen wall cupboards. Fluorescent tubes are cheap to run.

Recessed lighting
These compact light fittings take halogen lamps.

General-purpose lighting
Most light fittings will take either standard GLS lamps or compact energy-saving fluorescents.

Compact fluorescent tube

Display alcoves illuminated with striplights

Striplights
Sold as architectural tubes, striplights are 30W or 60W tubular tungsten-filament lamps with a metal cap at each end. They are often used for lighting inside cupboards, wardrobes and display cabinets. The semi-concealed light fittings can be controlled by separate microswitches so the light comes on only when the cupboard door is opened. To save more energy, replace them with fittings that take small fluorescent tubes.

Compact fluorescent tubes
Compact fluorescent lamps are designed as low-energy replacements for GLS bulbs. Though they are relatively expensive to buy, you are likely to recoup the additional cost within 6 to 12 months, thanks to the lower running costs. Low-energy lamps are available in both bayonet and edison-screw fittings, and should fit most light fittings. One disadvantage of these lamps is the time they take to reach their maximum level of brightness. This is not a problem in a room where the light is left on for long periods, but they may not be suitable in a movement-activated porch light, for example, where good instant illumination is required.

Light-emitting diodes (LEDs)
Formerly used only for indicator lights on electronic equipment, LEDs are now often used in groups to create extremely durable light sources. At present there are relatively few domestic light fittings made with LEDs, but their extremely long life expectancy suggests they could have a considerable impact on lighting design in the future.

The chart opposite compares the features and efficiency of various bulbs and tubes.

Comparing bulbs and tubes

• Lumens per watt – the higher the figure, the greater the efficiency (more light per unit of electricity). • Colour temperature (in degrees Kelvin) – the higher the figure, the colder (bluer) the light.		Common names	Normal range	Life expectancy in hours	Features	Typical lumens per watt	Colour temperature
General service lamp		Light bulb	40–150 watts	1000–2000	General-purpose bulbs in a range of shapes and colours.	12–18	2800
Decorative GLS		Candle, globe	25–60 watts	1000–2000	Bulbs designed to be visible.	7–12	2800
Crown-silvered lamp		Mirrored bulb	40–100 watts	1000–2000	Front of the bulb is coated to bounce light back against a reflective surface inside the light fitting.	8	2700
Internal-silvered lamp		Spotlamp	25–100 watts	1000–2000	The bulb is coated internally to reflect the light forward in a concentrated beam.	8–12.5	2800
Parabolic aluminized reflector		PAR	60–120 watts	1000–2000	Conical-shape reflector, often used for floodlighting.	8–13	3050
Architectural tube		Striplight	25–60 watts	1000–2000	Used to illuminate interior of cabinets and mounted above kitchen worktops.	7–12	2700
Fluorescent tube			13–125 watts	6000–7000	Gives bright, even illumination. A variety of warm and cool tones. Economical to run.	35–100	2700 to 6300
Compact fluorescent tube		Low-energy bulb	48–69 watts	6000–7000	Miniature tubes with Edison screw or bayonet fittings. Cheap to run, lasting 10 to 12 times longer than equivalent GLS bulbs.	6–30	2700 to 6300
Mains-voltage halogen lamp			20–50 watts	2000–4000	Less 'sparkle' than low-voltage halogen, but simpler to install. Popular for wall lights and recessed lighting.	12–16	3050
Linear mains-voltage halogen lamp		Double-ended halogen	100–500 watts	2000–4000	Mainly used for uplighters and floodlights. Tends to get very hot.	18–22	3050
Low-voltage halogen lamp			10–50 watts	2000–4000	Widely used for wall lights and recessed ceiling lights. Can be suspended from special plastic-insulated cable.	14–19	2900 to 3000
Light-emitting diode		LED	Up to 10 watts per light fitting	100,000	Often used for decorative fittings. Can be built into CCTV cameras. Does not get hot.	30–35	5500

SEE ALSO > Lower running costs 35

Collecting waste water

Why waste treated drinking water on the garden or by flushing it down the WC? Either collect the rainwater that runs off your roof or recycle water drained from your bath, shower, washbasins and washing machine.

Saving rainwater

If you want to save rainwater for your garden, fit a plastic diverter into a downpipe and connect it, via a filler tube, to an adjacent water butt.

How the diverter works

There are various diverters available, but they all work on similar principles. Water running down the inside of the downpipe is collected in a circular channel and diverted into a filler tube that runs to the water butt. When the butt is full, the channel overflows into the lower section of the downpipe.

Fitting a diverter is a straightforward job. Decide where you want the filler pipe, mark and cut the downpipe (**1**) and slip the diverter into place (**2**). Then connect the filler tube to it (**3**).

Section through rainwater diverter
1 Water in downpipe
2 Circular channel
3 Filler tube
4 Overflowing water

1 Remove a short section of the downpipe

2 Fit the diverter into the downpipe

3 Connect the filler pipe to the diverter

Collecting water on a larger scale

If you have the space, you can divert rainwater to collection tanks that have the capacity to store thousands of litres of water. Being much larger and heavier than the average water butt, storage tanks are usually buried underground or tucked away behind a garage or outbuilding. Underground tanks, in particular, are best installed by a contractor, and in most cases this is generally more convenient when combined with a new building project. The harvested rainwater can be pumped directly to individual WC cisterns or to your washing machine. Alternatively, you could have the water pumped to a separate storage tank in the loft, which can be connected to all your cisterns and your washing machine and to an outdoor tap from which you can water your plants and wash your car.

The underground storage tank can be connected to the mains water supply, so that it's topped up in the summer months when it could begin to run dry. The system will always utilize the free harvested rainwater in preference to mains water, which you have to pay for. According to the Water Regulations, there must be provision to prevent any possible contamination of the mains water supply. Before considering this type of back-up connection, check with your local authority that it meets with their approval.

Collecting grey water

A different system allows you to reuse 'grey water' – the water drained from basins, baths and showers. This is complicated by having to install a settlement tank and additional filters to remove contaminants, and the water has to be treated to deal with organic waste. It is also important to calculate fairly accurately the projected usage of grey water, because it should not be stored for longer than 24 hours in case it becomes a breeding ground for bacteria. Reusing water drained from the kitchen sink is not recommended.

Attempting to connect existing drainage to a grey-water storage system would be difficult, which is why it is only really economical to consider installation as part of a larger building project.

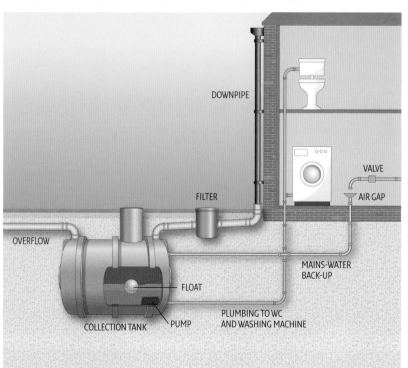

Rainwater-collection tank connected to WC and washing machine

SEE ALSO > Simple ways to conserve water 14

Plumbing systems

The system of plumbing that delivers hot and cold water to every tap, cistern and storage tank in your home may seem complicated if you have never tried to repair or maintain it yourself. However, a little time spent familiarizing yourself with your own plumbing could pay dividends.

The advantages of DIY plumbing

Being able to tackle your own plumbing installations and repairs can save you the cost of hiring professionals – and that can amount to a substantial sum of money. It also avoids the distress and inconvenience of ruined decorations, and the expense of replacing rotted household timbers where a slow leak has gone undetected. Then there's the saving in water. A dripping tap wastes litres of water a day – and if it's hot water, there's the additional expense of heating it. A little of your time and a few pence spent on a washer can save you pounds.

Water systems

Generally, domestic plumbing incorporates two systems. One is the supply of fresh water from the 'mains', and the other is the waste or drainage system that disposes of dirty water. Both of the systems can be installed in different ways.

Stored-water system (Indirect)

The majority of homes are plumbed with a stored-water supply system. The storage tank in the loft and the cold-water tap in the kitchen are fed directly from the mains; so possibly are your washing machine, electric shower(s) and outside tap. But water for baths, washbasins, flushing WCs and some types of shower is drawn from the storage tank, which should be covered with a purpose-made lid to protect the water from contamination. Drinking water should only be taken from the cold-water tap in the kitchen.

Cold water from the storage tank is fed to a hot-water cylinder, where it is indirectly heated by a boiler or immersion heater to supply the hot taps. The water pressure at the taps depends on the distance ('head') from the tank to the tap.

A stored-water system provides several advantages. There is adequate water to flush sanitaryware during a temporary mains failure; the major part of the supply is under relatively low pressure, so the system is reasonably quiet; and because there are fewer mains outlets, there is less likelihood of impure water being siphoned back into the mains supply.

Mains-fed system (Direct)

Many properties now take all their water directly from the mains – all the taps are under high pressure, and they all provide water that's suitable for drinking. This development has come about as a result of limited loft space that precludes a storage tank and the introduction of non-return check valves, which prevent drinking water being contaminated. Hot water is supplied by a combination boiler or a multipoint heater; these instantaneous heaters are unable to maintain a constant flow of hot water if too many taps are running at once. Some systems use an unvented, pressurised cylinder, which stores hot water but is fed from the mains.

A mains-fed system is cheaper to install than an indirect one. Other advantages include mains pressure and drinking water at all taps. With a mains-fed system there's no plumbing in the loft to freeze.

Drainage

Waste water is drained in one of two ways. In houses built before the late 1950s, water is drained from baths, sinks and basins into a waste pipe that feeds into a trapped gully at ground level. Toilet waste feeds separately into a large-diameter vertical soil pipe that runs directly to the underground main drainage network.

With a single-stack waste system, which is installed in later buildings, all waste water drains into a single soil pipe – the one possible exception being the kitchen sink, which may drain into a gully.

Rainwater usually feeds into a separate drain, so that the house's drainage system will not be flooded in the event of a storm.

• Wiring Regulations
When making repairs or improvements to your plumbing, make sure you don't contravene the electrical Wiring Regulations. All metal plumbing has to be bonded to earth. If you replace a section of metal plumbing with plastic, it is important to reinstate the earth link. (See below.)

Reinstate the link
If you replace a section of metal plumbing with plastic, you may break the path to earth – so make sure you reinstate the link. Bridge a plastic joint in a metal pipe with an earth wire and two clamps. If you are in any doubt, consult a qualified electrician.

SEE ALSO > Simple ways to conserve water 14, Repairing leaking taps 42–3

Draining the system

You will have to drain at least part of any plumbing system before you can work on it; and if you detect a leak, you will have to drain the relevant section quickly. So find out where the valves, stopcock and draincocks are situated, before you're faced with an emergency.

Saving hot water
If your gate valve won't close off and you don't want to drain all the hot water, you can siphon the water out of the cold tank with a garden hosepipe. While the tank is empty, replace the old gate valve.

Draining cold-water taps and pipes

• Turn off the main stopcock on the rising main to cut off the supply to the kitchen tap (and to all the other cold taps on a direct system).
• Open the tap until the flow ceases.
• To isolate the bathroom taps, close the valve on the appropriate cold-feed pipe from the storage tank and open all taps on that section. If you can't find a valve, rest a wooden batten across the tank and tie the arm of the float valve to it. This will shut off the supply to the tank, so you can empty it by running all the cold taps in the bathroom. If you can't get into the loft, turn off the main stopcock, then run the cold taps.

Draining hot-water taps and pipes

• Turn off immersion heater or boiler.
• Close the valve on the cold-feed pipe to the cylinder and run the hot taps. Even when the water stops flowing, the cylinder will still be full.
• If there's no valve on the cold-feed pipe, tie up the float-valve arm, then turn on the cold taps in the bathroom to empty the storage tank. (If you run the hot taps first, the water in the tank will flush all the hot water from the cylinder.) When the cold taps run dry, open the hot taps. In an emergency, open hot and cold taps to clear the pipes as quickly as possible.

Draining a WC cistern

• To empty the WC cistern itself, tie up its float-valve arm and flush the WC.
• To empty the pipe that supplies the cistern, either turn off the main stopcock on a direct system or, on an indirect system, close the valve on the cold feed from the storage tank. Alternatively, shut off the supply to the storage tank and empty it through the cold taps. Flush the WC until no more water enters its cistern.

Draining the cold-water storage tank

• To drain the storage tank located in the roof space, close the main stopcock on the rising main, then open all the cold-water taps in the bathroom. Bail out the residue of water at the bottom of the storage tank.

Draining the hot-water cylinder

Closing a float valve
Cut off the supply of water to a storage tank by tying the float arm to a batten.

• If the hot-water cylinder springs a leak (or you wish to replace it), first turn off the immersion heater and boiler, then shut off the cold feed to the cylinder from the storage tank (or drain the cold-water storage tank – see above). Run hot water from the taps.
• Locate a draincock from which you can drain the water remaining in the cylinder. It is probably located near the base of the cylinder, where the cold feed from the storage tank enters. Attach a hose and run it to a drain or sink that is lower than the cylinder. Turn the square-headed spindle on the draincock till you hear water flowing.
• Water can't be drained if the washer is baked onto the draincock seating, so disconnect the vent pipe and insert a hosepipe to siphon the cylinder.
• Should you want to replace the hot-water cylinder, don't disconnect all its pipework until you have drained the cylinder completely. If the water is heated indirectly by a heat-exchanger, there will be a coil of pipework inside the hot-water cylinder that is still full of water. This coil can be drained via the stopcock on the boiler after you have shut off the mains supply to the small feed-and-expansion tank in the roof space. Switch off the electricity to the central-heating system.

Adding extra valves

Unless you divide up the system into relatively short pipe runs with valves, you will have to drain off a substantial part of a typical plumbing installation even for a simple washer replacement.

• Install a gate valve on both the cold-feed pipes running from the cold-water storage tank. This will eliminate the necessity for draining off litres of water in order to isolate pipes and appliances on the low-pressure cold- and hot-water supply.
• When you are fitting new taps and appliances, take the opportunity to fit miniature valves on the supply pipes. In future, when you have to repair an individual tap or appliance, you will be able to isolate it in moments.

Gate valve
Fit a gate valve to the cold-feed pipes from the storage tank.

Miniature valve
Fit a miniature valve to the supply pipes below a sink or basin.

Sealed central-heating systems

A sealed system (see SEALED CENTRAL-HEATING SYSTEMS) does not have a feed-and-expansion tank – the radiators are filled from the mains via a flexible hose known as a filling loop. The indirect coil in the hot-water cylinder is drained as described left, though you might have to open a vent pipe that is fitted to the cylinder before the water will flow.

SEE ALSO > Sealed central heating 57, Radiators 59

Repairs and maintenance

It pays to master the simple techniques required for repairs and maintenance in order to prevent costly leakages from taps and sanitaryware. You will also avoid the expense of calling out a plumber, possibly at short notice. In addition, you may prevent water damage to your home and possessions.

Draining and refilling the system

Partially drain the plumbing system if you are leaving the house unoccupied for a few days during winter and leave the central heating on a low setting. For longer periods away at any time of the year, it's wise to drain the system completely.

Attach hosepipe to draincock

Partial drain-down
• Add special antifreeze to the central-heating feed tank and set the heating to come on briefly twice a day.
• Turn off the main stopcock.
• Open all taps to drain the system.

Full drain-down
• Switch off and extinguish the water heater and/or boiler.
• Turn off the main stopcock and, if possible, the main stopcock outside.
• Open all taps to drain the pipework.
• Open the draincock at the base of the hot-water cylinder. If there are draincocks in the rising main or other pipework, open them too.
• Flush the WCs.
• Drain the boiler and radiator circuits at the lowest points on the pipe runs.
• Add salt to the WC pan to prevent the trap water freezing.

Refilling the system
• Close all taps and draincocks.
• Turn on the main stopcock.
• Turn on taps and allow water and air to escape. Bleed radiators and check that float valves are working properly.

Thawing frozen pipes

If water won't flow from a tap during cold weather, or a tank refuses to fill, a plug of ice may have formed in one of the supply pipes. The plug cannot be in a pipe supplying taps or float valves that are working normally, so you should be able to trace the blockage quickly. In fact, freezing usually occurs first in the roof space.

As copper pipework transmits heat quickly, use a hairdryer to gently warm the suspect pipe, starting as close as possible to the affected tap or valve and working along it. Leave the tap open, so water can flow normally as soon as the ice thaws. If you can't heat the pipe with a hairdryer, wrap it in a hot towel or hang a hot-water bottle over it.

Preventive measures
Insulate pipework and fittings to stop them freezing, particularly those in the loft or under the floor. If you're going to leave the house unheated for a long time during the winter, drain the system (see left). Cure any dripping taps, so leaking water doesn't freeze in your drainage system overnight.

Thawing a frozen pipe
Play a hairdryer gently along a frozen pipe, working away from the blocked tap or valve.

Dealing with a punctured pipe

Unless you are absolutely sure where your pipes run, it is all too easy to nail through one of them when fixing a loose floorboard. You may be able to detect a hissing sound as water escapes under pressure, but more than likely you won't notice your mistake until a wet patch appears on the ceiling below, or some problem associated with damp occurs at a later date. While the nail is in place, water will leak relatively slowly, so don't pull it out until you have drained the pipework and can repair the leak. If you pull out the nail by lifting a floorboard, replace the nail immediately.

If you plan to lay fitted carpet, you can paint pipe runs on the floorboards to avoid such accidents in future.

Patching a leak

During freezing conditions, water within a pipe turns to ice, which expands until it eventually splits the walls of the pipe or forces a joint apart. The only other reason for leaking plumbing is mechanical failure – either through deterioration of the materials or because a joint has failed and is no longer completely watertight. Make a permanent repair if you can by inserting a new section of pipe or replacing a leaking joint (if it is a compression joint that has failed, try tightening it first). If you have to make an emergency repair, drain the pipe first. If it is frozen, make the repair before it thaws.

Sealing a split or pinhole
For a temporary repair, use a repair clamp, below, or special amalgamating tape which will work in wet conditions.

A push-fit repair pipe (see right), makes a fast, permanent repair if you have to remove a section of pipe.

Alternatively, a slip-on compression fitting (below left) will also make a permanent repair.

A push-fit repair pipe

A slip-on compression fitting makes a secure repair

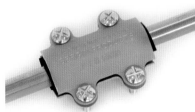

Fit an emergency repair clamp over the split

SEE ALSO >Insulating pipes 17

Repairing leaking taps

Leaking taps aren't too difficult to deal with. When water drips from a spout, it usually points to a faulty washer. If the tap is old, its seat may be worn, too. If water leaks from beneath the head of the tap when it's in use, the O-ring needs replacing. When you are working on a tap, insert the plug and lay a towel in the bottom of the washbasin, bath or sink to catch small objects and protect the surface.

Replacing a washer

To replace the washer in a traditional pillar tap, first drain the supply pipe, then open the valve as far as possible.

If the tap is shrouded with a metal cover, unscrew it by hand or use a wrench, taping the jaws to protect the chrome finish.

Lift the cover to reveal the headgear nut just above the body of the tap. Slip a spanner onto the nut and unscrew it (**1**).

The jumper to which the washer is fixed fits into the bottom of the headgear. In some taps the jumper is removed along with the headgear (**2**), but in other types it will be lying inside the tap body.

The washer itself may be pressed over a small button in the centre of the jumper (**3**) and can be prised off with a screwdriver. A securing nut can be hard to remove. Allow penetrating oil to soften any corrosion; then, hold the jumper stem with pliers and unscrew the nut with a spanner (**4**). If the nut sticks, replace the jumper and washer; otherwise, fit a new washer and retaining nut, then reassemble the tap.

Traditional pillar tap
The components of a pillar tap
1 Capstan head	**6** Jumper
2 Metal shroud	**7** Washer
3 Gland nut	**8** Tap body
4 Spindle	**9** Seat
5 Headgear	**10** Tail

1 Loosen headgear nut

2 Lift out headgear

3 Prise off washer

4 Or undo securing nut

Curing a dripping ceramic-disc tap

Getting inside a tap
On some taps the head and cover is in one piece. You will have to remove it to expose the headgear nut. Often a retaining screw is hidden beneath the coloured hot/cold disc in the centre of the head. Prise out the disc with the point of a knife or a small screwdriver (**1**). If there's no retaining screw, simply pull the head off (**2**).

1 Prise out the disc

2 Pull the head off

1 Unscrew and examine the valve

3 Unscrew retaining nut

2 Replace a worn rubber seal

4 Replace inlet seals

Ceramic-disc taps should be maintenance free, but faults can still occur. Since there's no washer to replace, you have to replace the whole valve when the tap leaks.

Turn off the water. Remove the headgear by turning it anticlockwise with a spanner. Remove the valve and examine it for wear or damage (**1**). Removing debris from the disc may do, but if disc is scratched, you will need a new valve. These are handed – left (hot), right (cold). Also examine the rubber seal on the bottom of the valve. If worn or damaged, it will cause the tap to drip. If need be, replace the seal with a new one (**2**).

Single-lever mixer taps have a cartridge that controls both flow and temperature. To replace it, remove handle cap. Use a socket spanner to undo the handle nut. Lift handle off, remove shroud and undo the cartridge-retaining nut (**3**), then lift out the cartridge. Fit new inlet seals on underside of cartridge if discs appear undamaged (**4**); replace the entire cartridge if they are visibly damaged.

SEE ALSO > Tap mechanisms 47

Repairing seats and glands

If replacing a washer doesn't solve the problem then the tap itself is probably worn. If you want to keep the taps, it is possible to renovate them.

Regrinding or renewing the seat

If a tap continues to drip after you have replaced the washer, the seat is probably worn, allowing water to leak past the washer. A simple way to cure this is to cover the old seat with a nylon liner that is sold with a matching jumper and washer (**1**). Drop the liner over the old seat, replace the jumper and assemble the tap. Close the tap to force the liner into position.

Alternatively, use a tap grinding tool (**2**) to put a new smooth surface on the seat. The tool uses serrated cutters to grind out any imperfections that might be allowing water past the washer.

With the headgear removed, insert the grinder (**3**) and screw the threaded bush to the tap to locate the tool securely.

Push down and twist the grinder clockwise. Resurfacing is complete when the whole seat is shiny and new looking.

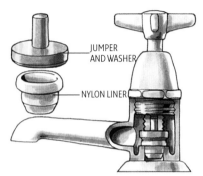

JUMPER AND WASHER

NYLON LINER

1 Repair a worn seat with a nylon liner

2 A tap grinding tool   **3 Cut new seat**

Stopcocks and valves

Stopcocks and gate valves are used rarely but often fail just when needed.

Make sure that they are operating smoothly by closing and opening them from time to time. Lubricate stiff spindles with penetrating oil. A stopcock is fitted with a standard washer, but as it is hardly ever under pressure it is unlikely to wear.

Penetrating oil or lubricant prevents seizure

Replacing O-rings

On a mixer tap each valve is usually fitted with a washer, as on conventional taps, but in most mixers the gland packing (see far right) has been replaced by a rubber O-ring. The base of a mixer's swivel spout is also sealed with a washer or O-ring. If water seeps from that, it needs replacing.

First remove the mixer spout – the retaining screw may be accessible from the front; if it's at the back, you may have to use a cranked screwdriver to remove it (**1**). Lift out the swivelling spout (**2**), then use a small screwdriver to prise out the O-ring from its groove (**3**). Take care not to scratch the metal. Lubricate a new ring with silicone grease (**4**), then carefully slide it into place before re-fitting the spout (**5**) and replacing the retaining screw.

1 Use a cranked screwdriver for rear screws

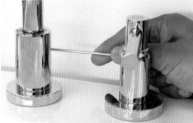

3 Remove the O-ring from the swivel spout

2 Lift out the swivelling spout

4 Lubricate a new O-ring

5 Replace spout

GLAND PACKING

Gland packing
Older-style taps are sealed with water-tight packing around the spindle.

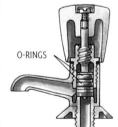

O-RINGS

O-ring seal
Modern taps are sealed with rubber rings, in place of gland packing.

SEE ALSO > Tap mechanisms 47

Maintaining cisterns and storage tanks

The mechanisms used in WC cisterns and storage tanks are probably the most overworked of all plumbing components, so servicing is required from time to time to keep them operating properly. You can get the spare parts you need from plumbers' merchants and DIY stores.

Direct-action WC cisterns

Most modern WCs are washed down by means of direct-action cisterns. Water enters the cistern through a valve, which is opened and closed by the action of a hollow float attached to one end of a rigid arm. As the water rises in the cistern, it lifts the float until the other end of the arm closes the valve and shuts off the supply.

Flushing is carried out by depressing a lever, which is linked by wire to a rod attached to a perforated plastic or metal plate at the bottom of an inverted U-bend tube (siphon). As the plate rises, the perforations are sealed by a flexible plastic diaphragm (flap valve), so the plate can displace a body of water over the U-bend to promote a siphoning action. The water pressure behind the diaphragm lifts it, so that the contents of the cistern flow up through the perforations in the plate, over the U-bend and down the flush pipe. As the water level in the cistern drops, so does the float – thus opening the float valve to refill the cistern.

Servicing cisterns

The few problems associated with this type of cistern are easy to solve. A faulty float valve or poorly adjusted float arm will allow water to leak into the cistern until it drips from the overflow pipe that runs to the outside of the house. Slow or noisy filling can often be rectified by replacing the float valve. If the cistern will not flush until the lever is operated several times, the flap valve probably needs replacing (see below). If the flushing lever feels slack, check that the wire link at the end of the flushing arm is intact. When water runs continuously into the pan, check the condition of the washer at the base of the siphon.

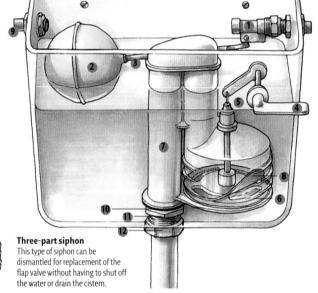

Direct-action cistern
The components of a typical direct-action WC cistern.
1 Float valve
2 Float
3 Float arm
4 Flushing lever
5 Wire link
6 Perforated plate
7 One-piece siphon
8 Flap valve
9 Overflow
10 Sealing washer
11 Retaining nut
12 Flush-pipe connector

Three-part siphon
This type of siphon can be dismantled for replacement of the flap valve without having to shut off the water or drain the cistern.

Miniature float valve
This type of float valve is designed for installing in WC cisterns only.

1 Wedge the float arm

2 Release flush pipe

3 Loosen retaining nut

4 Lift off flap valve

Replacing a flap valve

If a WC cistern will not flush first time, take off the lid and check that the lever is actually operating the flushing mechanism. If that appears to be working normally, then try replacing the flap valve in the siphon. Before you service a one-piece siphon, shut off the water by wedging the float arm with a bent wire across the cistern (**1**). Flush the cistern.

Use a wrench to unscrew the nut that holds the flush pipe to the underside of the cistern (**2**). Move the pipe to one side.

Release the retaining nut that clamps the siphon to the base of the cistern (**3**). A little water will run out as you loosen the nut – so have a bucket handy. You may find that the siphon is bolted to the base of the cistern, instead of being clamped by a single retaining nut.

Disconnect the flushing arm, then ease the siphon out of the cistern. Lift the diaphragm off the plastic plate (**4**) and replace it with one of the same size. Reassemble the entire mechanism and reconnect the flush pipe to the cistern.

Making a new wire link

You won't be able to flush a WC cistern if the flushing lever has come adrift.

Make a replacement for a rusted link from thick wire; if the lever connecting the handle to the link has broken, the WC can be flushed by pulling the wire link upwards until you can get a new one.

Curing continuous running water

If you notice that water is running into the pan continuously, turn off the supply and let the cistern drain. If the siphon hasn't split, try changing the sealing washer.

If the water is flowing from the float valve so quickly that the siphoning action is not interrupted, fit a float-valve seat with a smaller water inlet.

SEE ALSO > Adjusting the float arm 46

Diaphragm valves

The pivoting end of the float arm on a diaphragm valve (known in the trade as a Part 2 valve) presses against the end of a small plastic piston, which moves the large rubber diaphragm to seal the water inlet.

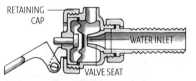

Diaphragm valve: retaining cap to the front

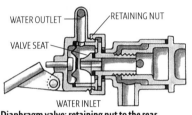

Diaphragm valve: retaining nut to the rear

Replacing the diaphragm

Turn off the water supply, then unscrew the large retaining cap. Depending on the model, the nut may be screwed onto the end of the valve or behind it (see above).

With the latter type of valve, slide out the cartridge inside the body (**1**) to find the diaphragm behind it. With the former, you will find a similar piston and diaphragm immediately behind the retaining cap (**2**).

Wash the valve, before assembling it along with the new diaphragm.

1 Slide out the cartridge to release the diaphragm

2 Undo the cap and pull float arm to find the valve

Close-coupled WCs and push-button cisterns

This modern style of WC does away with the pipe that connects the cistern to the pan. Water flows from the cistern through a moulded-in channel in the pan to the rim. The cistern is bolted directly to the pan and a rubber seal prevents leaks at the joint. This style often features compact cisterns with push-button action and lower water usage.

The cistern may incorporate a diaphragm valve, but it's becoming more common to find close-coupled WCs with push-button, 'continental'-style cisterns. Here, the traditional handle is replaced by a button on the top of the cistern. Usually the button is split, to give a dual flush facility of 4 or 6 litres (7 or 10½ pints), helping to save water.

Push-button cisterns use a different type of valve, which is activated via a cable release. A small float controls the level of water in the cistern. The valve usually incorporates an overflow, which allows water to flow into the toilet bowl – rather than outside via an overflow pipe – if there is a problem.

The mechanism inside the cistern is all plastic, so won't rust. As a result, there's less to go wrong, but if problems occur spare parts may be harder to find as there are many different types available.

These cisterns produce a faster flush, which doesn't give the same cleansing action as a slower, syphon-operated flush. However, they are quiet in operation and allow for a very slimline cistern, helping to reduce the 'footprint' of the WC.

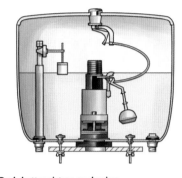

Push-button cistern mechanism

A close-coupled cistern with push-button operation

Other types of cistern valve

A Fluidmaster valve converts a lever-operated siphon into a push-button cistern. A flap valve controls the flow of water into the WC. Quiet in use and water-efficient, it works well with low-capacity cisterns, but is not suitable for double-trap toilets. Two kits are available: one which replaces the lever and siphon; the other which also replaces the float valve.

The Torbeck valve can be used to replace the diaphragm or piston valve in most cisterns. Its all-plastic construction means there's nothing to corrode. After flushing, water enters the cistern through a tube which is mostly below water level, so there's no noise from splashing. The float is easily adjustable via a screw thread. Side and bottom entry versions are available, the latter with a built-in debris filter and flow control device.

Flapper valve
This is a modern replacement for the siphon and can be operated by handle or push-button. It helps to save water because it only allows water to flush while the handle or button is depressed, unlike a siphon, which empties a full cistern every time. It has a built-in overflow, but as it lies in the bottom of the cistern it can be prone to lime scale or debris interfering with the seal. It can be used in conjunction with all types of float valve.

Fluidmaster valve

Torbeck valve

SEE ALSO > Turning off the water 40, Adjusting the float arm 46

Renovating valves and floats

A cistern or tank that doesn't work properly can prevent WCs flushing properly or cause noise throughout the plumbing system. Sorting the problem can be as simple as bending the float arm or adjusting a screw.

Adjusting the float arm

Adjust the float so as to maintain the optimum level of water, which is about 25mm (1in) below the outlet of the overflow pipe.

Bend the metal arm on a Portsmouth valve downward to reduce the water level, or straighten it to let in more water (1).

The arm on a diaphragm valve has an adjusting screw, which raises or lowers the arm to alter the water level (2).

1 Straighten or bend a metal float arm

Thumb-screw adjustment
Some float arms are cranked, and the float is attached with a thumb-screw clamp. To adjust the water level in the cistern, slide the float up or down the rod.

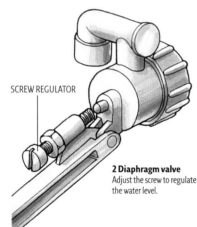

Float valve with flexible silencer tube

SCREW REGULATOR

2 Diaphragm valve
Adjust the screw to regulate the water level.

Replacing the float

Modern plastic floats rarely leak, but old-style metal floats eventually corrode and allow water to seep into the ball. The float gradually sinks, until it won't ride high enough to close the valve. Unscrew the float to see if there is water inside.

If you can't obtain a new float for several days, lay the ball on a bench, enlarge the leaking hole with a screwdriver and pour out the water. Cover the ball with a plastic bag, tying the neck tightly around the float arm, and then replace the float.

Curing noisy cisterns

Cisterns that fill noisily can be very annoying. It was once permitted to screw a pipe into the outlet of a valve so that it hung vertically below the level of the water. This solved the splashing problem, but concern about the possibility of water 'back-siphoning' through the silencer tube into the mains supply led to rigid tubes being banned in favour of flexible plastic silencer tubes (see far left), which seal by collapsing should back-siphoning occur.

A silencer tube can also prevent water hammer – a rhythmic thudding that reverberates along the pipework. This is often the result of ripples on the surface of the water in a cistern, caused by a heavy flow from the float valve. As the water rises, the float arm bouncing on the ripples 'hammers' the valve, and the sound is amplified and transmitted along the pipes. A flexible plastic tube will stop ripples by introducing water below the surface.

If the pressure through the valve is too high, the arm oscillates as it tries to close the valve – causing water hammer. This can be cured by fitting an equilibrium valve. As water flows through the valve, some of it is introduced behind the piston or diaphragm to equalize the pressure on each side, so that the valve closes smoothly and silently.

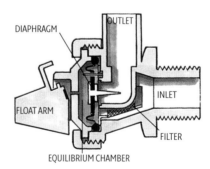

DIAPHRAGM
OUTLET
INLET
FLOAT ARM
FILTER
EQUILIBRIUM CHAMBER

Diaphragm-type equilibrium valve

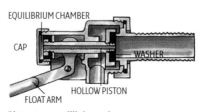

EQUILIBRIUM CHAMBER
CAP
WASHER
HOLLOW PISTON
FLOAT ARM

Piston-type equilibrium valve

Renewing a float valve

Turn off the supply of water to the cistern or tank, then use a spanner to loosen the tap connector joining the supply pipe to the float-valve stem. Remove the float arm, then unscrew the fixing nut outside of the cistern and pull out the valve.

Fit the replacement valve and, if possible, use the same tap connector to join it to the supply pipe.

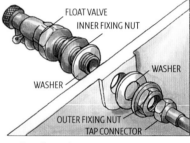

FLOAT VALVE
INNER FIXING NUT
WASHER
WASHER
OUTER FIXING NUT
TAP CONNECTOR

Renewing a float valve
Clamp the valve to the cistern with fixing nuts.

Choosing the correct pressure

Float valves are made to suit different water pressures: low, medium and high (LP, MP and HP). If the pressure is too low for the valve, the cistern may take a long time to fill; if too high, it may leak continuously. Most domestic WC cisterns require an LP valve; those fed direct from the mains need an HP valve. If the head (the height of the tank above the float valve) is greater than 13.5m (45ft), fit an MP valve; if over 30m (100ft), fit an HP valve. In an apartment with a packaged plumbing system (a storage tank built on top of the hot-water cylinder), the pressure may be so low that you will have to fit a full-way valve to the WC cistern in order to get it to fill reasonably quickly. If you live in an area where water pressure fluctuates a great deal, fit an equilibrium valve (see left).

To alter the pressure of a modern valve, simply replace the seat inside.

SEE ALSO > Float valves 45

Replacing taps

You may need to replace your taps for a number of reasons. Perhaps the present taps are beyond repair, or you simply want a change of style. On the other hand, you might want to substitute taps that reduce the amount of water that is wasted each time you turn on a conventional tap.

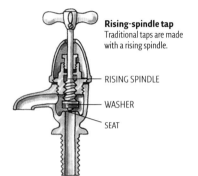

Rising-spindle tap
Traditional taps are made with a rising spindle.

RISING SPINDLE

WASHER

SEAT

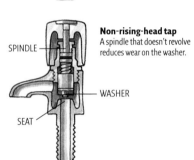

Non-rising-head tap
A spindle that doesn't revolve reduces wear on the washer.

SPINDLE

WASHER

SEAT

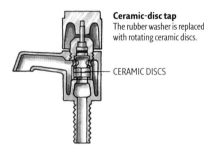

Ceramic-disc tap
The rubber washer is replaced with rotating ceramic discs.

CERAMIC DISCS

Types of tap

Conventional taps fall into three categories: rising-spindle taps, non-rising-head taps and ceramic-disc taps.

The first two are both fitted with rubber washers that are compressed, shutting off the flow of water when you turn the spindle clockwise. When a washer wears, the tap leaks.

With the third category, precision-ground ceramic discs are used in place of the traditional rubber washer. One disc is fixed and the other rotates until the waterways through them align and water flows. There is minimal wear, as hard-water scale or other debris is unlikely to interfere with the close fit of the discs. In practice, very little maintenance is required with this type of tap but, if a problem does develop, the entire inner cartridge and the lower seal can be replaced.

Single-action mixer taps

The majority of washbasins are fitted with individual taps for hot and cold water. Running water from two individual taps often results in excess water being used as you try to balance the temperature in the basin. The mechanism within a single-lever mixer tap tends to reduce wastage by balancing the flow rate and temperature of

the water before it emerges from the spout. Some single-lever taps have a mechanism that resists the upward movement of the lever, restricting the flow rate until you deliberately override the mechanism to produce full flow.

Spray taps

Aerating taps introduce air into the water. creating a gentle bubbling flow that is soothing to the touch.

A similar effect can be created when the nozzle is fitted with a plate pierced all over with tiny holes that break the water into droplets. This restriction at the nozzle increases pressure while reducing flow rate. Spray taps tend to clog more easily in hard-water areas.

Self-closing and sensor taps

Electronic sensors that turn the tap on when you place your hands beneath the spout are commonplace in commercial establishments. So are self-closing taps that are operated manually, but switch themselves off after a short period. Although they are likely to be relatively expensive to buy, there is no reason why you should not have such taps in your new bathroom or cloakroom.

The right pressure
Some taps imported from the Continent have relatively small inlets and are intended for use with mains-pressure supply only. These taps will not work efficiently if they are connected to a low-pressure tank-fed supply.

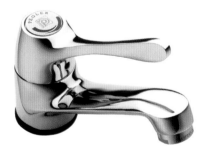

Basin taps
(top left)
Single lever mixer tap

(bottom left)
Self-closing tap

(far right)
Electronic sensor tap

Single-lever mixer tap
Moving the lever up and down turns the water on and off. Swinging it from one side to the other alters the temperature, by mixing hot water with cold. These taps have smaller, 10mm (³⁄₈in) feed pipes, which will need adaptors to connect to 15mm (¹⁄₂in) supply pipes.

SEE ALSO > Repairing taps 42–3, Fitting taps 48

Removing old taps

When replacing taps, you will want to use the existing plumbing if possible, but disconnecting old, corroded fittings can be difficult.

Apply some penetrating oil to the tap connectors and to the back-nuts that clamp the tap to the basin. While the oil takes effect, shut off the cold and hot water supply to the taps.

If necessary, apply heat with a gas torch to break down the corrosion – but wrap a wet cloth around nearby soldered joints, or you may melt the solder. Take care that you do not damage plastic fittings and pipes, and protect flammable surfaces with a ceramic tile. Try not to play the flame onto a ceramic basin.

Cranked spanners

It is not always possible to engage the nuts with a standard wrench. Instead, use a special cranked spanner designed to reach into the confined spaces below a basin or bath. You can apply extra leverage to the spanner by slipping a stout metal bar or wrench handle into the other end.

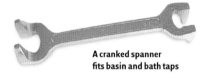

A cranked spanner fits basin and bath taps

Removing a stuck tap

Even when you have disconnected the pipework and back-nut, you may find that the taps are stuck in place with putty. Break the seal by striking the tap tails lightly with a wooden mallet. Clean the remnants of putty from around the holes in the basin, then fit new taps. If the tap tails are shorter than the originals, buy special adaptors designed to take up the gaps.

Releasing a tap connector
Use a special cranked spanner to release the fixing nut of a tap connector.

Fitting new taps

If you're installing a new bath or basin, it's much easier to fit the taps before the sanitaryware is in position since access to hard-to-reach nuts will be much better.

Most taps are made to standard sizes, so you shouldn't have any difficulty with new baths or basins, but if you're replacing the taps on an older fitting, check that they will cover the holes adequately or, if you're using a two-hole tap, fit in the holes.

Check that the spout is long enough to deliver water properly – there must be enough overhang to wash your hands underneath a basin tap, for instance.

Basin taps

Taps are supplied with flexible anti-rotation washers to stop the tap moving as it is turned on or off. Slip the washer onto the tap tail (**1**) and insert the tap through the hole (it is customary to put the hot tap on the left). Add the back-nut (**2**) then hold the tap steady as you tighten

1 Slip the anti-rotation washer over the tap tail

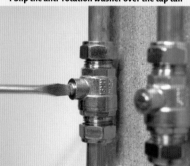

3 Service valves make future maintenance easy

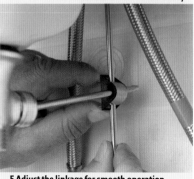

5 Adjust the linkage for smooth operation

it with a cranked spanner.

While you have the water turned off, fit service valves so that the taps can be serviced in future without having to turn off the water. These can be fitted in the supply pipe or you can get versions that double as tap connectors (**3**).

Single-hole mixer taps usually come with small-bore flexible hose tails (**4**), which make connecting the supply pipes much easier.

Some mixers feature a control that operates a pop-up waste. Adjust the rods carefully to ensure (**5**) that the plug seats and lifts correctly.

Bath taps

Two-hole mixers are fitted in much the same way as basin taps. If you're fitting *in situ*, remove the overflow fitting to give you more access. Mixers are supplied with flexible washers to seal the holes – if the washer colour doesn't suit your decor, use silicone sealant instead (**6**).

2 Add the back nut

4 Flexible pipes make fitting simple

6 Bed the tap in silicone sealant

SEE ALSO > Turning off the water 40, Types of tap 47

Choosing a shower

All showers, except for the most powerful models, use less water than required for filling a bath. And because showering is generally quicker than taking a bath, it helps to alleviate the morning queue for the bathroom. For even greater convenience, install a second shower somewhere else in the house – this is one of those improvements that really does add value to your home. Many appliances are superficially similar in appearance, so it's important to read the manufacturers' literature carefully before you opt for a particular model.

Pressure and flow

When choosing a shower, bear in mind that pressure and flow are not the same thing. For example, an instantaneous electric shower delivers water at high mains pressure, but a relatively low flow rate is necessary to allow the water to heat up as it passes through the shower unit.

A conventional gravity-fed system delivers hot water from a storage cylinder under low pressure, but often has a high flow rate when measured in litres per minute. Adding a pump to this type of system can increase both pressure and flow rate. Alter the flow and pressure ratio by fitting an adjustable showerhead with a choice of spray patterns, from needle jets to a gentle 'champagne' cascade .

This showerhead provides a choice of spray patterns

Gravity-fed showers

In most homes cold water is stored in a tank in the loft and fed to a hot-water cylinder at a lower level. Both the hot-water and cold-water pressures are determined by the height (or 'head') of the cold-water storage tank above the shower. A minimum head of at least 1m (3ft) should give a reasonable flow rate and pressure. If flow and pressure are insufficient for a good shower, you could improve the situation by raising the tank or fitting a pump in the system.

Mains-pressure showers

Some types of shower are fed directly from the mains: one of the simplest to install from a plumbing point of view is an instantaneous electric shower, although it will need a dedicated electricity supply.

Another alternative is to install a thermal-store cylinder. Mains-pressure water passes through a rapid heat exchanger inside the cylinder (see right). Yet another option is to store hot water in an unvented cylinder – which will supply high-pressure water to a shower without the need for a booster pump.

Nowadays showers are often supplied from combination boilers, though these often need to run at full flow to keep the boiler firing properly. Before buying a shower, check with the manufacturer of your boiler to ascertain whether there's likely to be a problem.

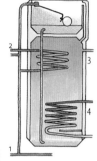

Thermal-store cylinder
Mains-fed water passes through a rapid heat exchanger on its way to the shower.
1 Mains feed
2 To shower
3 Other outlets
4 Boiler connections

Shower enclosures
If space permits, choose an enclosed shower cubicle (centre left). However, there are a number of screens and plumbing options, which make an over-the-bath shower almost as efficient.

Drainage

Draining the used water away from a shower can be more of a problem than running the supply.

If it is not possible to run the waste pipe between the floor joists or along a wall, then you may have to consider relocating the shower. In some situations it may be necessary to raise the shower tray on a plinth in order to gain enough height for the waste pipe to fall (slope) towards the drain. Another way to overcome the problem is to install a special pump to take the waste water away from the shower.

Shower traps

When running the waste pipe to an outside hopper, you can fit a conventional trap – but these are relatively large, creating problems when installing the shower tray.

You could cut a hole in the floor, or substitute either a smaller, shallow-seal or compact trap that includes a removable grid and dip tube for easy cleaning. Another possibility is to fit a running trap in the waste pipe at a convenient location, or install a self-sealing valve in the pipe.

A shower trap that is connected to a soil stack must have a water seal not less than 50mm (2in) deep. The best solution is to fit a compact trap, which is shallow enough to fit under most modern shower trays, but is designed to provide the necessary water seal. Otherwise, fit either a running trap or a self-sealing valve.

Wet rooms
Wet rooms do away with shower trays and have drainage through the floor. They create a clean, uncluttered look, but need careful waterproofing to avoid problems with leaks

SEE ALSO > Shower mixers and sprayheads 50, Thermal-store cylinders 53, Unvented cylinders 53

Shower mixers and sprayheads

Basic shower mixers are little more than specialized taps – some tend to waste more water than others. For greater convenience and to reduce water usage, choose thermostatic mixers and look for sprayheads that are designed specifically to restrict the flow of water.

Bath/shower mixers

This type of shower is the simplest to install. It is connected to the existing 22mm (¾in) hot and cold pipes in the same way as a standard bath mixer, and the bath's waste system takes care of the drainage. Once you have obtained the right temperature at the spout by adjusting the hot and cold valves, you lift a button on the mixer, or turn a lever, to divert the water to the sprayhead via a flexible hose. The sprayhead can be hung from a wall-mounted bracket to provide a conventional shower, or hand-held for washing hair.

Because the supply pipes for this type of shower are part of the overall house system, it's impossible to guard against fluctuating pressure – and potentially scalding temperatures – unless the mixer is fitted with a thermostatic valve. An unregulated shower could be a real hazard if there are very young or elderly residents. Installing a pressure-equalizing valve in the pipework will add convenience and safety – if the pressure is insufficient, fit a booster pump.

Don't fit a bath/shower mixer unless both the hot and cold water is under the same pressure, either high or low.

This type of shower has controls that are uncomfortably low to reach.

Manual shower mixers

A manual shower mixer can be located over a bath or in a separate shower cubicle. Manual mixers require their own independent hot and cold supply.

Simple versions are available with individual hot and cold valves. But most manual shower mixers have a single control that regulates the flow and temperature of the water, and this type of mixer wastes less water than those with separate hot and cold valves. Single-lever ceramic-disc mixers operate exceptionally smoothly and, having few moving parts, are less prone to hard-water scaling.

You can choose a surface-mounted unit, or a nearly flush mixer with the pipework, connections and shower mechanism all concealed in the wall.

Bath/shower mixer
Fit this type of shower unit like an ordinary bath mixer.

Dual-lever mixer
With this type of mixer, one lever controls flow and the other temperature.

Thermostatic mixers

A thermostatic shower mixer is similar in design to a manual mixer, but it has an extra control incorporated to preset the water temperature. If the flow rate drops on either the hot or cold supply, a thermostatic valve rapidly compensates by reducing the flow on the other side. This is primarily a safety measure, to prevent the shower user being scalded should someone run a cold tap elsewhere in the house. A thermostatic shower should be supplied by means of branch pipes from the bathroom plumbing – but try to join them as near as possible to the cold tank and hot cylinder. The mixer can't raise the pressure of the supply, so you still need a booster pump if the pressure is low.

Thermostatic mixer mechanisms are usually based on wax-filled cartridges or bimetallic strips. Brand-new thermostatic valves respond extremely quickly to changes of temperature, but the rate slows down as scale gradually builds up inside the mixer. Even when new, reaction time will be slower if the mixer is expected to cope with exceptionally hot water (above 65°C/149°F). At such high temperatures the hot-water ports are almost fully closed and the cold ones almost wide open, so there is little margin for more adjustment.

The majority of thermostatic mixers can be used with an existing gravity-fed hot and cold supply, but it may be necessary to fit a booster pump. Check the manufacturer's literature – some showers don't perform well at low pressures.

Thermostatic mixer
This unit prevents excessive fluctuations in water temperature.

Sprayheads

There's a wide range of sprayheads available and many are adjustable to offer a variety of spray patterns. In addition to the standard shower spray, a simple adjustment is all that is needed to produce an invigorating pulsing jet to wake you up in the morning or a soft bubbly stream that saves water. The gentler delivery is ideal for small children. Some sprayheads can also be adjusted to deliver a very light spray while you soap yourself or apply shampoo.

Water-saving showerheads may not be suitable for instantaneous electric showers, which could overheat.

Rubber nozzles
Rub the the rubber nozzles on a modern sprayhead occasionally with your hand to help shift lime scale.

Cleaning a sprayhead

Gradually, accumulation of lime scale blocks the holes in the sprayhead and eventually this affects the performance of your shower. The harder the water, the more often it will need cleaning.

Remove the entire sprayhead from its hose or unscrew the perforated plate from the showerhead. Leave the sprayhead or plate to soak in a proprietary descalant until the scale has dissolved, then rinse thoroughly under running cold water.

Before you reattach the sprayhead or plate, turn on the shower to flush any loose scale deposits from the pipework.

SEE ALSO > Types of tap 47, Choosing a shower 49

Instantaneous showers

An instantaneous electric shower is designed specifically for connection to the mains water supply, using a single 15mm (½in) branch pipe from the rising main. A non-return valve must be fitted close to the unit.

Incoming water is heated within the unit, so there is no separate hot-water supply to balance. The shower is thermostatically controlled to prevent fluctuations in pressure affecting the water temperature and will switch off completely if there is a serious pressure failure. Some units have a shut-down facility – when you switch off, the water continues to flow for a little while to flush any hot water out of the pipework. This ensures that someone stepping into the cubicle immediately after another user isn't subjected to an unexpectedly hot start to their shower.

The electrical circuit

An instantaneous shower requires a separate circuit from the consumer unit. A ceiling-mounted double-pole switch is connected to the circuit to turn the appliance on and off.

Surface-mounted or concealed

With most instantaneous showers, all plumbing and electrical connections are contained in a single mixer cabinet that is mounted in the shower cubicle or over the bath. However, you can buy showers with a slim, flush-fitting control panel that is connected via a low voltage cable to a power pack installed out of sight – for example, under the bath behind a screw-fixed panel.

Fit a stopcock or miniature isolating valve in the supply pipe to allow the shower to be serviced.

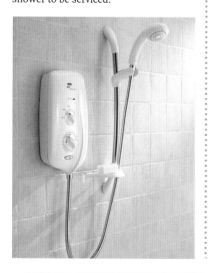

Pump-assisted showers

The pump-assisted 'power' shower is many people's concept of the ideal shower, but its water consumption is extremely high. And because it draws both hot and cold water, there's the cost of heating the water to consider. Turn off the shower when applying soap and shampoo.

Most power showers need a head of about 75 to 225mm (3 to 9in) to activate the pump when the mixer control is turned on. A pump can be used to boost the pressure and flow rate of stored hot and cold water, but not mains-fed water.

Ideally, the cold supply should be taken directly from the storage tank – not from branch pipes that feed other taps and appliances. The hot-water supply can be connected to the cylinder by means of a Surrey or Essex flange, which helps to eliminate the tendency for the pump to suck in air from the vent pipe.

If the water is heated by an electric immersion heater, make sure the cylinder is fed by a dedicated cold feed and that the cold-feed gate valve is fully open. This is to prevent the top of the cylinder running dry and perhaps burning out the heater. If the cylinder is heated from a boiler, make sure the water temperature is controlled by a thermostat. If the water is too hot, the shower could splutter.

Many power showers resemble instantaneous units, with the mixer controls and pump enclosed in a waterproof casing mounted on the shower cubicle wall.

Other pumps are designed for remote installation in the pipes feeding the shower mixer. These freestanding pumps can also be used to improve the performance of an existing installation. They're usually located next to the hot-water cylinder in an airing cupboard – as low as possible, so that the pump remains full of water. There are also pumps that are designed to perform satisfactorily when mounted at a high level – even in a loft. In such situations, a single-impeller pump is best.

Water Regulations

If the shower is mounted in such a way that the sprayhead could dangle below the rim of the bath or shower tray, you have to fit double-seal non-return valves in the supply pipes to prevent dirty water being siphoned back into the system. Most shower sets come with a bracket to prevent the hose reaching that far.

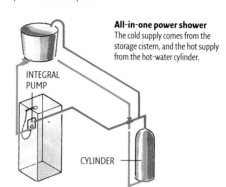

All-in-one power shower
The cold supply comes from the storage cistern, and the hot supply from the hot-water cylinder.

INTEGRAL PUMP

CYLINDER

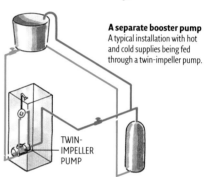

A separate booster pump
A typical installation with hot and cold supplies being fed through a twin-impeller pump.

TWIN-IMPELLER PUMP

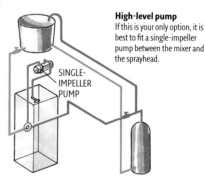

High-level pump
If this is your only option, it is best to fit a single-impeller pump between the mixer and the sprayhead.

SINGLE-IMPELLER PUMP

Computer-controlled showers

Computerized showers allow for the precise selection of temperature and flow rates, using a touch-sensitive control panel. Most control panels also include a memory program, so that each member of a family can select their own preprogrammed ideal shower.

These showers have real advantages for the disabled and for elderly people since they are exceptionally easy to operate – and the control panel can even be mounted outside the cubicle, so that it's possible to warm up the shower before you get in, or operate it for someone else.

Touch-sensitive computerized panel

SEE ALSO > Simple ways to conserve water 14

Heating water

In most houses, the hot water is heated and stored in a large copper vented cylinder situated in the airing cupboard. Cold water is fed to the base of the cylinder from the cold-water storage tank housed in the loft. As the water is heated, it rises to the top of the cylinder, where it is drawn off via a branch from the vent pipe to the hot taps. When the hot water is run off, it is replaced by cold water at the base of the cylinder, ready for heating.

Typical pipe runs
Red: Hot water
Blue: Cold water

Direct water heating by means of a boiler

Indirect water heating employs the central-heating boiler

The vent pipe itself runs back to the loft, where it passes through the lid of the cold-water storage tank, with its open end just above the level of the water. The vent pipe provides a safe escape route for air bubbles and steam, should the system overheat.

When water is heated, it expands. The vent pipe accommodates some of this water, but much of it is forced back up the cold-feed pipe into the cold storage tank.

Methods of heating water in the cylinder

There are two different methods of heating the water stored in a vented hot-water cylinder. Either directly – usually by electric immersion heaters – or indirectly, by means of a heat exchanger connected to the central-heating system.

Direct heating
Water heating can be accomplished solely by means of electric immersion heaters – either a single-element or double-element heater is fitted in the top of the cylinder, or there may be two individual side-entry heaters.

An alternative is for the water to be heated in a boiler that's used solely for supplying hot water for the cylinder. A cold-water pipe runs from the base of the cylinder to the boiler, where the water is heated; and it then returns to the top half of the cylinder.

Both methods are known as direct systems. In practice, a boiler-heated cylinder is generally fitted with an immersion heater as well, so that hot water can be supplied independently during the summer, when using the boiler would make the room where it is situated uncomfortably warm.

Indirect heating
When a house is centrally heated with radiators fed by a boiler, the water in the cylinder is usually heated indirectly by a heat exchanger. Hot water from the boiler passes through the exchanger (a coiled tube within the cylinder), where the heat is transmitted to the stored water. The heat exchanger is part of a completely self-contained system, which has its own feed-and-expansion tank (a small storage tank in the loft) to top up the system. An open-ended vent pipe terminates over the same small tank.

The whole system is known as the primary circuit, and the pipes running from and back to the boiler are known as the primary flow and return. An indirect system is often supplemented with an immersion heater.

Hot-water cylinders

The capacity of domestic cylinders normally ranges from about 114 litres (25 gallons) to 227 litres (50 gallons), although it is possible to obtain bigger cylinders. A cylinder with a capacity of between 182 and 227 litres (40 and 50 gallons) will store enough hot water to satisfy the needs of an average family for a whole day.

Some cylinders are made from thin, uninsulated copper and need to have a thick lagging jacket to reduce heat loss. However, for better performance use a Kite-marked factory-insulated cylinder that is precovered with a thick layer of foamed polyurethane.

Changing a cylinder

You may wish to replace an existing cylinder because it has sprung a leak, or because a larger one will allow you to take full advantage of cheap night-time electricity by storing more hot water. A simple replacement can sometimes be achieved without modifying the plumbing, but you'll have to adapt the pipework to fit a larger cylinder.

If you plan to install central heating at some point in the future, you can plumb in an indirect cylinder fitted with a double-element immersion heater and simply leave the heat-exchanging coil unconnected for the time being.

Place the new cylinder in position and check the existing pipework for alignment. Modify the pipes as need be, then make the connections, using PTFE tape to ensure that the threaded joints are watertight. Fit a draincock to the feed pipe from the tank, if there isn't one already installed. Fill the system and check for leaks before you heat the water, and check again when the water is hot.

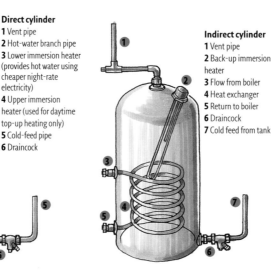

Direct cylinder
1 Vent pipe
2 Hot-water branch pipe
3 Lower immersion heater (provides hot water using cheaper night-rate electricity)
4 Upper immersion heater (used for daytime top-up heating only)
5 Cold-feed pipe
6 Draincock

Indirect cylinder
1 Vent pipe
2 Back-up immersion heater
3 Flow from boiler
4 Heat exchanger
5 Return to boiler
6 Draincock
7 Cold feed from tank

SEE ALSO > Lagging 17, Draining the system 40

Unvented cylinders

An unvented cylinder supplies mains-pressure hot water throughout the house. This is achieved by connecting the cylinder directly to the rising main. Most manufacturers recommend a 22mm (3/4in) incoming pipe, but a 15mm (1/2in) main at high pressure is normally adequate. An unvented cylinder can be heated directly, using immersion heaters; or indirectly, provided you are not using a solid-fuel boiler.

Unvented cylinder

There are no storage tanks, feed-and-expansion tanks, or open-vent pipes associated with unvented cylinders. Instead, a diaphragm inside a pressure vessel mounted on top of the cylinder flexes to accommodate expanding water. If the vessel fails, an expansion-relief valve protects the system by releasing water via a discharge pipe.

There are several other safety devices associated with unvented cylinders. A normal thermostat should keep the temperature of the water in the cylinder below 65°C (150°F). If it reaches 90°C (195°F), then a second thermostat will either switch off the immersion heater or shut off the water supply from the boiler. Finally, if it should get as hot as 95°C (205°F), a temperature-relief valve opens and discharges water outside.

Bylaws and regulations

The installation of an unvented hot-water cylinder needs to comply with both the Water Regulations and the Building Regulations. It has to include all the necessary safety devices and be installed by a competent fitter, such as those registered with the Institute of Plumbing, the Construction Industry Training Board, or the Association of Installers of Unvented Hot Water Systems (Scotland and Northern Ireland). Have the installation serviced regularly by a similarly qualified fitter, to make sure all the equipment remains in good working order.

You must notify your water company and local Building Control Office if you intend to fit an unvented hot-water cylinder.

Thermal-store cylinder

A thermal-store cylinder reverses the indirect principle. Water heated by a central-heating boiler passes through the cylinder and transfers heat, via a highly efficient coiled heat exchanger, to mains-fed water supplying hot taps and showers. An integral feed-and-expansion tank is normally built on top of the cylinder.

When the system is working at maximum capacity, the mains-fed water is delivered at such a high temperature that cold water must be added via a thermostatic mixing valve plumbed into the outlet supplying taps and showers. As the cylinder is exhausted, less cold water is added. The thermal-store system provides mains-pressure hot water throughout the house, dispenses with the need for a cold-water storage tank in the loft, and increases the efficiency of the boiler.

A valve is needed to prevent the heat from the cylinder 'thermo-siphoning' (gravity circulating) around the central-heating system. This can be a motorized valve or a simple mechanical gravity-check (non-return) valve that is opened by the force of the central-heating pump.

As with all open-vented systems, the feed-and-expansion tank determines the head of water, and radiators must be lower than the tank in order to be filled with water. When the tank is combined with the cylinder, it needs to be situated on the top floor of the house in order to provide central heating throughout the building. If that is impossible, install a tankless thermal-store cylinder in your chosen location and fit a conventional feed-and-expansion tank in the loft.

A thermal-store cylinder

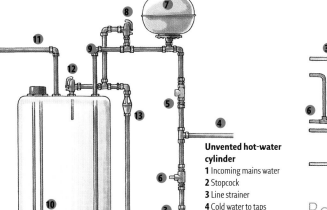

Unvented hot-water cylinder
1 Incoming mains water
2 Stopcock
3 Line strainer
4 Cold water to taps
5 Non-return (check) valve
6 Pressure limiter
7 Pressure vessel
8 Expansion-relief valve
9 Cold-water inlet
10 Immersion heater
11 Hot-water outlet
12 Temperature-relief valve
13 Air break (tundish)
14 Discharge pipe

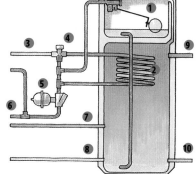

Thermal-store cylinder
1 Integral feed-and-expansion tank
2 Heat-exchanger
3 Supply pipe to hot taps/shower
4 Thermostatic mixing valve
5 Expansion vessel
6 Mains feed
7 Space-heating flow
8 Space-heating return
9 Boiler flow
10 Boiler return

Benefits of unvented systems

Thermal-store cylinders help to reduce boiler cycling and, because they heat water more quickly, can cut fuel usage by up to 15 per cent. Their capacities range from 80 to 210 litres (17½ to 46 gallons) and the systems can deliver flow rates of between 18 and 30L/min (31½ and 52½ pints). Unvented systems heat quickly and their high levels of insulation mean low heat losses. High flow rates in excess of 30L/min (52½ pints) are achievable.

Solar energy

There are systems designed to harness solar energy that offer an effective alternative for heating domestic water or can at least make a considerable contribution towards the cost. In contrast to the demand for space heating, which varies according to the season, hot water is required constantly throughout the year; and it is well suited to heating by means of solar energy.

Using solar energy to heat water

Mount collectors on a south-facing roof

The idea of using the sun to provide free, non-polluting energy for heating water has always appealed to conservationists, but thanks to soaring energy costs and technological developments solar power is becoming increasingly popular.

There are two main types of solar panel: solar collectors, which absorb energy from the sun and use it to heat water; and photovoltaic or solar electric panels, which convert solar radiation directly into electricity. Solar collectors are of most use in the home and there are two types: flat plate and evacuated tubes.

Flat plate collectors can be a simple sheet of metal painted black that absorbs the sun's energy. Water is fed through the panel in pipes attached to the metal sheet (a central heating radiator is often used in DIY panels) and picks up the heat in the metal. The metal sheet is embedded in an insulated box and covered with glass or clear plastic on the front.

The evacuated tube system is more expensive and uses a series of glass heat tubes grouped together. The tubes are highly insulated, due to a vacuum inside the glass. From the late spring through to early autumn, this type of system can produce a useful proportion of the household hot water. During the winter, the solar collectors provide useful 'preheat' that reduces the time it takes a boiler to heat water, thereby saving energy.

There are a number of companies that supply solar collectors for heating water, plus all the controls and pipework required to complete the job. If you carry out the plumbing yourself, the payback on the investment will be that much greater.

Ideally, a solar panel should be mounted on a south-facing roof at a 30° angle to the horizontal and out of reach of shadows from trees, buildings or chimneys.

A basic system

Most systems for supplying domestic hot water will require solar collectors that cover about 4sq m (4sq yd) of roof space. In order to trap maximum heat from the sun, the collectors should be mounted on a south-facing pitched roof. Collectors can be fitted, with minimal structural alterations, to almost any building, and planning approval is rarely required.

The most common way of utilizing solar energy to boost an existing water-heating system is to feed the hot water from the collectors to a second heat exchanger fitted inside your hot-water cylinder. This usually means replacing the cylinder with a dual-coil model.

An alternative technique is to plumb in a second well-insulated cylinder, which will 'preheat' the water before it is passed on to the main storage cylinder. This may involve raising the cold-water storage tank in order to feed the new preheat cylinder.

Controls

A pump is needed to circulate the water from the collectors to the cylinder coil and back to the collectors. A programmable thermostat, which operates the pump, senses when the panels are hotter than the water in the cylinder.

Point-of-use water heaters

Electric point-of-use water heaters are often designed to fit inside a cupboard or vanity unit beneath a sink or basin. You can install one of these heaters yourself, provided that it has a capacity of less than 9 litres (16 pints). Follow the manufacturer's instructions precisely, and fit a pressure-limiting valve and a filter (both of these are supplied as a kit). Also, make sure that the safety vent pipe discharges hot water to a place outside where it won't endanger anyone.

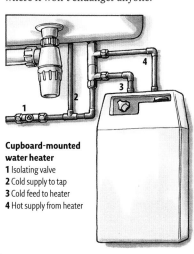

Cupboard-mounted water heater
1 Isolating valve
2 Cold supply to tap
3 Cold feed to heater
4 Hot supply from heater

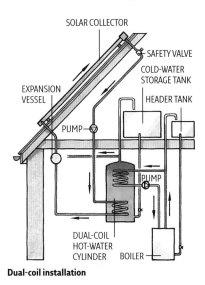

Dual-coil installation

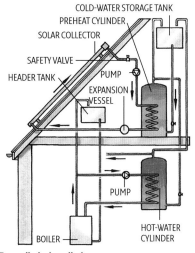

Two-cylinder installation

Efficient heating

Central heating is the most efficient method for keeping your house warm, but you can waste a great deal of heat if you don't control the system effectively. Your fuel bills will escalate unless there are thermostats to keep the temperature down to the optimum level – and it would be grossly uneconomical to heat your home when you're out at work, or at night when you are tucked up snugly in bed.

You also need to maintain the system to get the best performance. If your radiators are full of air or clogged up with corrosion, they won't be giving off the amount of heat they should – and consequently the thermostat will switch on the boiler more often in an attempt to bring the ambient temperature up to the level you require.

It also helps to have your boiler serviced regularly. If you find that your old boiler is no longer up to the job, check with your local authority to see if you are eligible for a grant towards its replacement.

Central heating

Of the various methods used over the years, central heating is the most energy-efficient, since it supplies heat from a single source (usually a boiler or furnace) to every room in the house, instead of the need for an individual heater or fireplace in each room. It is also relatively easy to maintain, because there is just the one heating appliance to control, clean and service.

Central-heating systems can be divided into two basic types: dry and wet systems. With the less-common dry system, heated air carries warmth to the rooms; with a wet system, the heat-carrying medium is water.

Dry central-heating systems

The heat source for the majority of warm-air central-heating systems is a large gas-fired furnace. Air is warmed by being passed relatively quickly over a metal heat exchanger containing hot gas fumes, which are eventually ducted to a flue. An integral fan blows the warmed air through ducts to the rooms being heated.

Each of these ducts ends in an adjustable damper, which is used to regulate the temperature in the room by controlling the amount of air that can flow through it. Ducting runs in this kind of system can be quite long and must be insulated for maximum efficiency.

There are also a number of electric systems that are regarded as forms of central heating. Among them are underfloor and ceiling heating systems. These use electric elements built into the structure of the floor or ceiling to warm their surfaces, which in turn radiate heat into the room.

A house kept warm with individual electric storage heaters is also usually classed as being centrally heated, even though each heater is a separate heat source. The individual heaters contain a number of heat-retaining firebricks, which are heated during the night by electric elements running on the low-cost Economy 7 electricity tariff. The units are individually controlled, so the bricks can give off the stored heat as required during the daytime – either by simple convection or with the aid of fans.

Choosing a system

Before you decide on a central-heating system, investigate which method is likely to work best for you – both in terms of installation and the long-term benefit and running costs.

Dry central heating
Because of the amount of space and work required to run the ducts, a ducted warm-air system is not really practical unless incorporated into a house during its construction. Similarly, electric underfloor and ceiling systems for whole-house heating are best put in while a house is being built or when you decide to add an extension to your home.

Room storage heaters can be easily installed in an existing house, although they need a dedicated meter, consumer unit and wiring.

Wet central heating
Wet central-heating systems have proved to be economical, reliable and relatively easy to install. Their small-bore copper or plastic pipes can be run through floor and ceiling voids, clipped along skirting boards and up walls to supply hot water to panel radiators or low-profile skirting heaters.

Most systems use two 15mm (½in) copper pipes (see opposite, top); micro-bore heating uses smaller, 6 to 10mm (¼ to ⅜in), pipes and offers faster warm-up and less heat loss.

Underfloor systems are efficient and space-saving. They use concealed plastic pipes to emit heat.

Modern compact boilers are highly efficient and can be installed in a fireplace, utility room or in the kitchen.

Wet systems will prove to be the most economical, flexible choice for the vast majority of householders; the new generation of 'designer' fixtures means that radiators can make an eye-catching focal point, too.

Warm-air systems
Heated air travels via ducts to the rooms, and then back to the furnace for reheating.

Floor and ceiling heating systems
Electric elements warm the floor or ceiling, and the heat is radiated into the room.

Storage heaters
These run on cheap electricity and have their own consumer unit, wiring and meter.

Wet central heating

Wet central heating is economic, efficient and reliable and by far the most common form of central heating. It offers relatively quick warm-up times and a variety of control options for flexibility and energy saving. Although it is prone to various problems, most of these are easily resolved in a well-designed system.

Open-vented systems

The most common form of wet central heating is the two-pipe open-vented system – in which water is heated by a boiler and pumped through small-bore pipes to radiators or convector heaters, where the heat from the water is released into the rooms. The water then circulates back to the boiler for reheating, using natural gas, bottled gas (propane), oil, electricity, or a solid fuel.

Thermostats and valves allow the output of the individual heat emitters to be adjusted automatically, and parts of the system can be shut down as required.

This type of system can be used to heat the domestic hot-water supply, as well as the house itself. Some older systems employ gravity circulation to heat the hot-water storage cylinder but incorporate an electric pump to force the water around the radiators. In most modern systems, a pump propels the water to the cylinder and radiators via diverter valves.

Sealed systems

A sealed system is an alternative to the traditional open-vented method. Water is fed into the system via a filling loop, which is temporarily connected to the mains. In place of a feed-and-expansion tank (see top right), a pressure vessel containing a flexible diaphragm accommodates the expansion of the water as the temperature rises. Should the system become overpressurized, a safety valve discharges some of the water.

There is less corrosion in a sealed system and, because it runs at a relatively high temperature, the radiators can be smaller. Because there's no feed-and-expansion tank installed in the loft, radiators can be placed anywhere in the house, including in the loft itself.

However, sealed systems must be completely watertight – since there is no automatic top up – and they have to be made with expensive, high-quality components to prevent pressure loss. A boiler with a high-temperature cutout is required, in case the ordinary thermostat fails. Also, radiators get very hot.

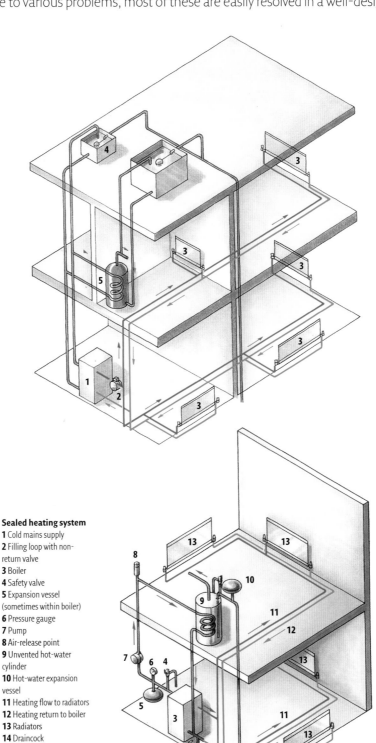

Open-vented system
The water heated by the boiler (**1**) is driven by a pump (**2**) through a two-pipe system to the radiators (**3**) or special convector heaters, which give off heat as the hot water flows through them, gradually warming the rooms to the required temperature; the water then returns to the boiler to be reheated. A feed-and-expansion tank (**4**), situated in the loft, keeps the system topped up and takes the excess of water created by the system overheating. The hot-water cylinder (**5**) is heated by gravity circulation. In the diagram, red indicates the flow of water from the pump and blue shows the return flow.

Sealed heating system
1 Cold mains supply
2 Filling loop with non-return valve
3 Boiler
4 Safety valve
5 Expansion vessel (sometimes within boiler)
6 Pressure gauge
7 Pump
8 Air-release point
9 Unvented hot-water cylinder
10 Hot-water expansion vessel
11 Heating flow to radiators
12 Heating return to boiler
13 Radiators
14 Draincock

● **One-pipe system**
In an outdated one-pipe system, heated water is pumped around the perimeter of the house through a single large-bore pipe that forms a loop. Flow and return pipes divert hot water to each radiator by means of gravity circulation. Larger radiators may be required at the end of the loop in order to compensate for heat loss. A one-pipe system incorporates a feed-and-expansion tank and a hot-water circuit similar to those used for conventional two-pipe systems.

Central-heating boilers

Technological improvements have made it possible to produce central-heating boilers that are smaller and more efficient than their predecessors. Today, gas and oil are still the most popular fuels because, despite advances in solid-fuel technology, the dirt and inconvenience associated with solid fuels can't be ignored or overcome. Wood-burning boilers aren't really practical for suburban homes, though a wood-fired stove could be used to heat a room, perhaps with a small back boiler to provide hot water.

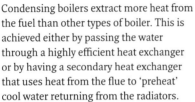

● Gas installers
Gas boilers must be installed by competent fitters registered with CORGI (Council for Registered Gas Installers). Check, also, that your installer has the relevant public-liability insurance for working with gas.

● Boiler flues
All boilers need some means of expelling the combustion gases that result from burning fuel. Frequently this is effected by connecting the boiler to a conventional flue or chimney that takes the gases directly to the outside.
    Alternatively, some boilers, known as room-sealed balanced-flue boilers, are mounted on an external wall and the flue gases are passed to the outside through a short horizontal duct. Balanced-flue ducts are divided into two passages – one for the outgoing flue gases, and the other for the incoming air needed for efficient combustion.
    All boilers can be connected to a conventional flue, but gas and oil-fired boilers are also made for balanced-flue systems. If the boiler is fan-assisted, it can be mounted at some distance – typically 3 or 4m (10 or 12ft) – from the balanced-flue outlet.

Condensing boilers

Condensing boilers extract more heat from the fuel than other types of boiler. This is achieved either by passing the water through a highly efficient heat exchanger or by having a secondary heat exchanger that uses heat from the flue to 'preheat' cool water returning from the radiators.

With a conventional boiler, the moisture within the exhaust gases passes through the flue as steam. In a condensing boiler, which extracts additional heat from the gases, the moisture condenses within the boiler and is drained through a pipe.

Building Regulations now require all new gas- and oil-fired boilers fitted in households to be of the condensing type, because of their low energy use, whether the installation is a new build or a replacement. More complex than a standard gas boiler, they are also more costly.

Strict rules apply on the location of the flue to avoid gases being vented across footpaths or under a neighbour's window, for instance. Your Building Control Officer will be able to advise.

Oil-fired boilers

Pressure-jet oil-fired boilers are fitted with controls similar to the ones for gas boilers described above. Oil boilers can be floor-standing or wall-mounted. Oil-fired heating requires a large external storage tank, with easy access for delivery tankers.

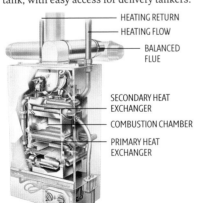

— HEATING RETURN
— HEATING FLOW
— BALANCED FLUE
— SECONDARY HEAT EXCHANGER
— COMBUSTION CHAMBER
— PRIMARY HEAT EXCHANGER

Condensing boiler

Gas-fired boilers

Older gas-fired boilers have pilot lights that burn constantly, in order to ignite the burners whenever heat is required. The burners may be operated manually or by a timer set to switch the heating on and off at selected times. The boiler can be linked to a room thermostat, so that the heating is switched on and off to keep temperatures at the required level throughout the house. Another thermostat inside the boiler prevents overheating.

An increasing number of boilers have energy-saving electronic ignition. The pilot is not lit until the room thermostat demands heat and cuts off once up to temperature.

Solid-fuel boilers

Solid-fuel boilers are invariably floor-standing and require a conventional flue. Back boilers are small enough to be built into a fireplace. The rate at which the fuel is burnt is controlled by a thermostatic damper or sometimes by a fan.

The system must have some means for the heat to escape in case of a circulation pump failure, or the water could boil, causing damage. This is usually in the form of a pipe that leads from the boiler and the heat exchanger in the domestic hot-water cylinder to a radiator situated in the bathroom, where the excess heat can be used to dry wet towels.

Some models have a hopper feed that tops them up automatically. You need a suitable place to store fuel for the boiler and the residual ash has to be removed regularly.

Combination boilers

Combination boilers provide both hot water to a sealed heating system and a separate supply of instant hot water directly to taps and showers. The advantages are ease of installation (no tanks or pipes in the loft), space-saving (no hot-water storage cylinder), economy (you heat only the water you use) and mains pressure at taps and shower heads.

The main drawback is a fairly slow flow rate, so filling a bath can take a long time and it's not usually possible to use two hot taps at the same time. Combination boilers are therefore best suited to small households or flats. However, to overcome these problems, the newer generation of combination boilers incorporate a small hot-water storage tank.

Heating requirements

The capacity (heat output) of the boiler needed can be calculated by adding up the specified heat output of all the radiators, plus a 3kW allowance for a hot-water cylinder. Ten per cent is added to allow for very cold weather. The overall calculation is affected by the heat lost through the walls and ceiling, and also by the number of air changes caused by ventilation.

Some plumbers' merchants will make the relevant calculations for you, if you provide them with the dimensions of each room. Alternatively, you can find calculators online.

The efficiency of a boiler is determined by its SEDBUK (Seasonal Efficiency of Domestic Boilers in the UK) rating from A to G. A-rated boilers are more than 90 per cent efficient.

SEE ALSO > Grants 7, Thermostats 34, 61

Ventilating a boiler

A boiler that takes its combustion air from within the house and expels fumes through a conventional open flue (see opposite far left) must have access to a permanent ventilator fitted in an outside wall. The ventilator has to be of the correct size – as recommended by the boiler manufacturer – and must not contain a fly-screen mesh, which could become blocked. Refer to Building Regulations F1-1.8 for specific guidance. A boiler that is starved of air will create carbon monoxide – a lethal invisible gas that has no smell.

A cupboard that houses a balanced-flue room-sealed boiler must be fitted with ventilators at the top and bottom, to prevent the boiler overheating.

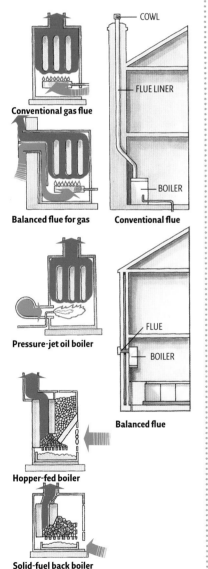

Conventional gas flue

Balanced flue for gas **Conventional flue**

COWL
FLUE LINER
BOILER

Pressure-jet oil boiler

FLUE
BOILER
Balanced flue

Hopper-fed boiler

Solid-fuel back boiler

Radiators

The hot water from a central-heating boiler is pumped along small-bore pipes connected to radiators, mounted at strategic points to heat individual rooms and hallways. The standard radiator is a double-skinned pressed-metal panel, which is heated by the hot water that flows through it.

Despite its name, a radiator emits only a fraction of its output as radiant heat – the rest being delivered by natural convection as the surrounding air comes into contact with the hot surfaces of the radiator. As the warmed air rises towards the ceiling, cooler air flows in around the radiator, and this air in turn is warmed and moves upwards. As a result, a very gentle circulation of air takes place in the room, and the temperature gradually rises to the optimum set on the room thermostat.

Panel radiators

Radiators are available in a wide range of sizes. The larger they are, the greater their heat output. Output for a given size can be increased further by using 'double radiators', which are made by joining two panels one behind the other. Most types of radiator have fins attached to their rear faces to induce convected heat.

The handwheel valve at one end of the radiator turns the flow of water on or off; the lockshield valve at the other end is set to balance the system, then left alone. An ordinary handwheel valve can be fitted at either end of a radiator, regardless of the direction of flow. However, thermostatic valves, which regulate the temperature of individual radiators, are marked with arrows to indicate the direction of flow and must be fitted accordingly.

A bleed valve is used to release air that can build up inside the radiator and prevent the panel from heating properly.

Decorative radiators
Radiators don't have to be white and flat. You could choose from modern takes on old-fashioned cast iron radiators, elegant vertical radiators in stainless steel, or curved, finned models designed for tight spaces or just to look good.

Double-panel radiator

Finned radiator

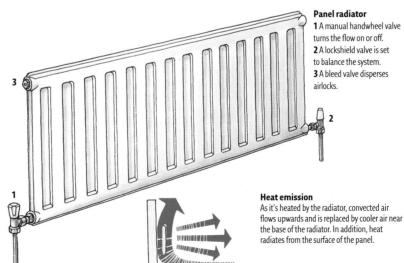

Panel radiator
1 A manual handwheel valve turns the flow on or off.
2 A lockshield valve is set to balance the system.
3 A bleed valve disperses airlocks.

Heat emission
As it's heated by the radiator, convected air flows upwards and is replaced by cooler air near the base of the radiator. In addition, heat radiates from the surface of the panel.

SEE ALSO > Reflective foil 17, Thermostatic valves 61, Bleeding radiators 65

Convectors and skirting radiators

Convectors and skirting radiators are a space-saving and more expensive alternative to panel radiators. Heat from hot water pumped through them is transferred to the air via fins or a panel, which replaces the skirting board in the room.

Convectors

Rising warm air draws in cool air below

Convector heaters can be used as part of a wet central-heating system. Some models are designed for inconspicuous fixing at skirting level.

Convectors emit none of their heat in the form of direct radiation. The hot water from the boiler passes through a finned pipe inside the heater, and the fins absorb the heat and transfer it to the air around them. The warmed air passes through a damper-controlled vent at the top of the heater, and at the same time cool air is drawn in through the open bottom to be warmed in turn.

With a fan-assisted convector heater, the airflow is accelerated over the fins in order to speed up room heating.

Skirting radiators

Fan-assisted convector
This unit makes good use of the wasted space under a kitchen unit.

A skirting radiator is a space-saving alternative to a conventional panel radiator and is designed for installation in place of a wooden skirting board. The twin copper-lined waterways and the outer casing are formed from a single aluminium extrusion (see below) and are clipped to the wall with a special bracket.

Made in various lengths up to 6m (19ft 6in) lengths and available in various finishes, skirting radiators are cut to length then joined at the corners of the room, using conventional soldered pipe joints. The pipework and valves are hidden from view, but are readily accessible for maintenance or repair.

Electric versions are also available.

Positioning convectors and radiators

At one time, central-heating radiators and convector units were nearly always placed under windows, because the area around a window tends to be the coldest part of a room. However, if you've fitted double glazing to reduce heat loss and draughts, then it will be more efficient to place heaters elsewhere – especially if windows are hung with long curtains.

Finned radiators offer a greater heat output and more flexibility in their siting. The shape of a room can also affect the siting of radiators and, perhaps, the number. For example, it is difficult to heat a large L-shaped room with just a single radiator at one end. In situations like this it's probably best to consult a heating installer to help you decide upon the optimum number and position of heaters.

Wherever possible, avoid hanging curtains or standing furniture in front of a radiator or convector heater. Curtains and furniture absorb radiated heat – and curtains also trap convected heat.

The warm air rising from a radiator will eventually discolour the paint or wall-covering above it. Fitting a narrow shelf about 50mm (2in) above a radiator avoids staining, without inhibiting convection. Alternatively, enclose the radiator in a decorative cover – heat output is barely reduced, provided air is able to pass through the enclosure freely, especially at the top and bottom (see below).

Radiator covers

Fitting a cover around a radiator will turn it into a decorative feature. The cabinet must be ventilated to allow air into the bottom and for the convected warm air to exit from the top. A perforated panel is usually fitted across the front to dissipate the heat and add to the unit's appearance.

Cabinets are available in kit form to fit standard-size radiators. Alternatively, you can make your own from MDF board.

Making your own cabinet
A radiator cabinet can be designed to stand on the floor or to be hung on the wall at skirting height. A floor-standing version is described here.

Cut the shelf (**1**) and two end panels (**2**) from 18mm (¾in) MDF. Make these components large enough to enclose the radiator and both valves.

Glue the panels to the shelf with dowel joints, and dowel a 50 x 25mm (2 x 1in) tie rail (**3**) between the sides at skirting level. Cut a new skirting moulding with a vent in the bottom edge (**4**) to fit along the base. Complete the box by applying a decorative moulding (**5**) around the edge of the shelf.

Cut a front panel (**6**) from either perforated hardboard, MDF, aluminium mesh or bamboo lattice, and mount it in a rebated MDF frame (**7**). Hold the frame in place with magnetic catches.

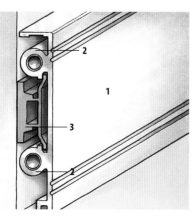

Skirting radiator
1 Aluminium extrusion
2 Copper-lined waterways
3 Mounting assembly

Floor-standing radiator cabinet
1 Shelf
2 End panel
3 Tie rail
4 Skirting
5 Moulding
6 Perforated panel
7 Frame

SEE ALSO ▶ Reflective foil 17, Radiators 59

Controls for central heating

There are various automatic control systems and devices available for wet central heating that bring greater control and can help cut running costs by reducing wastage of heat to a minimum. Automatic controllers can be divided into three basic types: temperature controllers (thermostats), automatic on-off switches (programmers and timers), and heating-circuit controllers (zone valves). These devices can be used, individually or in combination, to provide a very high level of control.

Thermostats

All boilers incorporate thermostats to prevent overheating. An oil-fired or gas boiler will have one that can be set to vary heat output by switching the unit on and off; and some models are also fitted with modulating burners, which adjust flame height to suit heating requirements. On a solid-fuel boiler, the thermostat opens and closes a damper that admits more or less air to the firebed to increase or reduce the rate of burning, as required.

A room thermostat – 'roomstat' for short – is often the only form of central-heating control fitted. It is placed in a room where the temperature usually remains fairly stable, and works on the assumption that any rise or drop in the temperature will be matched by similar variations throughout the house.

Roomstats control the temperature by means of simple on-off switching of the boiler – or the pump, if the boiler has to run constantly in order to provide hot water. The main drawback of a roomstat is that it can't sense temperature changes in other rooms – caused, for example, by the sun shining through a window or a separate heater being switched on.

More sophisticated temperature control is provided by a thermostatic valve, which can be fitted to a radiator instead of the standard manually operated valve. A temperature sensor opens and closes the valve, varying the heat output to maintain the desired temperature in the individual room. Thermostatic radiator valves need not be fitted in every room, but could reduce the heat in a kitchen or spare bedroom, for example, while a roomstat regulates the temperature in the rest of the house.

The most sophisticated thermostatic controller is a boiler-energy manager or 'optimizer', which collects data from sensors inside and outside the building in order to deduce the optimum running period so the boiler is not wastefully switched rapidly on and off.

Boiler-energy manager

Room thermostat

Programmer or timer

Thermostatic radiator valve

Heating controls
There are a number of ways to control heating:
1 A wiring centre connects the controls in the system.
2 A programmer/timer is used in conjunction with a zone valve to switch the boiler on or off at preset times, and run the heating and hot-water systems.
3 Optional boiler-energy manager controls the efficiency of the heating system.
4 Room thermostats are used to control the pump, or zone valves to regulate the overall temperature.
5 A non-electrical thermostatic radiator valve controls the temperature of an individual heater.

Zone-control valves

In most households the bedrooms are unoccupied for much of the day, so don't need heating continuously.

One way of avoiding such waste is to divide your central-heating system into circuits or 'zones' (upstairs and downstairs, for example) and to heat the whole house only when necessary. If you zone your house, make sure the unheated areas are adequately ventilated, to prevent condensation.

Control is via motorized valves linked to a timer or programmer that directs the heated water through selected pipes at predetermined times of the day. Alternatively, zone valves linked to individual thermostats can be used to provide separate temperature control for each zone.

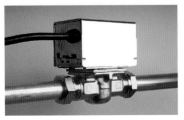

A motorized zone-control valve

Timers and programmers

You can cut fuel bills substantially by ensuring that the heating is not on while you are out or asleep. A timer can be set so that the system is switched on to warm the house before you get up and goes off just before you leave for work, then comes on again shortly before you return home and goes off at bedtime. The simpler timers provide two 'on' and two 'off' settings, which are normally repeated every day. A manual override enables you to alter the times for weekends and other changes in routine.

More sophisticated devices, known as programmers, offer a larger number of on-off programs – even a different one for each day of the week – as well as control of domestic hot water.

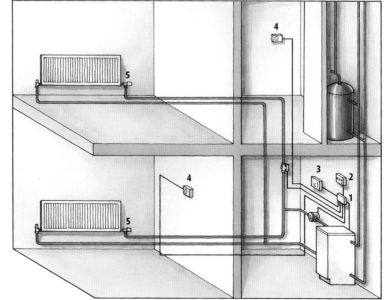

Diagnosing heating problems

When heating systems fail to work properly, they can exhibit all sorts of symptoms, some of which can be difficult to diagnose without specialized knowledge and experience. However, it pays to check out the more common faults, summarized below, before calling out a heating engineer.

Hissing or banging sounds from boiler or heating pipes

This is caused by overheating due to:

• **Blocked chimney (if you have a solid-fuel boiler)** Sweep chimney to clear heavy soot.

• **Build-up of scale due to hard water** Shut down boiler and pump. Treat system with descaler. Drain, flush and refill system.

• **Faulty boiler thermostat** Shut down boiler. Leave pump working to circulate water, to cool system quickly. When it's cool, operate boiler thermostat control. If you don't hear a clicking sound, call in an engineer.

• **Lack of water in system** Shut down boiler. Check feed-and-expansion tank in loft. If empty, the valve may be stuck. Move float-valve arm up and down to restore flow and fill system. If this has no effect, check to see if mains water has been turned off by accident or (in winter) if supply pipe is frozen.

• **Pump not working** Shut down boiler, then check that pump is switched on. If pump is not running, turn off power and check wired connections to it. If pump seems to be running but outlet pipe is cool, check for airlock by opening pump bleed screw. If pump is still not working, shut it down, drain system, remove pump and check for blockage. Clean pump or, if need be, replace it, preferably with the same model for ease of installation.

Radiators in one part of the house do not warm up

• **Timer or thermostat that controls relevant zone valve is not set properly or is faulty** Check timer or thermostat setting and reset if need be. If this has no effect, switch off power supply and check wired connections. If that makes no difference, replace unit.

• **Zone valve is faulty** Replace motor or drain system and replace entire valve.

• **Pump not working** *See above.*

All radiators remain cool, though boiler is operating normally

• **Pump not working** Check pump by listening or feeling for motor vibration. If pump is running, check for airlock by opening bleed valve. If this has no effect, the pump outlet may be blocked. Switch off boiler and pump, remove pump and clean or replace as necessary. If pump is not running, switch off and try to free spindle. Look for a large screw in the middle – removing or turning it will reveal the slotted end of the spindle. Turn this until the spindle feels free, then switch the pump on again.

• **Pump thermostat or timer is set incorrectly or is faulty** Adjust thermostat or timer setting. If that has no effect, switch off power and check wiring connections. If they are in good order, call in an engineer.

Area at top of radiator stays cool

• **Airlock at top of radiator is preventing water circulating fully** Bleed radiator to release trapped air.

Single radiator doesn't warm up

• **Handwheel valve is closed** Open the valve.

• **Thermostatic radiator valve is set too low or is faulty** Adjust valve setting. If this has no effect, drain the system and replace the valve.

• **Lockshield valve not set properly** Remove lockshield cover and adjust valve setting until radiator seems as warm as those in other rooms. Have lockshield valve properly balanced when the system is next serviced.

• **Radiator valves blocked by corrosion** Close both radiator valves, remove radiator and flush out.

Cool patch in centre of radiator

• **Deposits of rust at bottom of radiator are restricting circulation of water** Close both radiator valves, remove radiator and flush out.

Boiler not working

• **Thermostat set too low** Check that roomstat and boiler thermostats are set correctly.

• **Programmer or timer not working** Check programmer or timer is switched on and set correctly. Replace if fault persists.

• **Gas boiler's pilot light goes out** Relight pilot following instructions supplied with boiler (these are usually printed on the back of the front panel). If pilot fails to ignite, have it replaced.

Continuous drip from overflow pipe of feed-and-expansion tank

• **Faulty float valve or leaking float, causing valve to stay open** Shut off mains water supply to feed-and-expansion tank and bale out to below level of float valve. Remove valve and fit new washer. Or, unscrew leaking float from arm and fit new one.

• **Leaking heat-exchanger coil in hot-water cylinder** Dripping from overflow will occur only if the feed-and-expansion tank is below the cold-water storage tank. Turn off boiler and mains water. Let system cool, then take dip-stick measurement in both tanks. Don't use water overnight – check again in morning. If water level has risen in the feed-and-expansion tank and dropped in the cold-water storage tank, replace hot water cylinder.

Water leaking from system

• **Loose pipe unions at joints, pump connections, boiler connections, etc.** Turn off boiler (or close down solid-fuel appliance) and switch off pump, then tighten leaking joints. If this has no effect, drain the system and remake joints.

SEE ALSO › Draining the system 40, Curing leaks 41, Float valves 44–6, Bleed valve 65, Removing a radiator 65

Draining and refilling

Although it's inadvisable to do so unnecessarily, there may be times when you have to drain your wet central-heating system completely and refill it. This could be for routine maintenance, when dealing with a fault, or because you have decided to extend the system or upgrade the boiler. The job can be done fairly easily if you follow the procedures outlined here.

Draining the system

Before draining your central-heating system, cool the water by shutting off the boiler and leaving the circulation pump running. The water in the system will cool quite quickly.

Switch off the pump and turn off the mains water supply to the feed-and-expansion tank in the loft either by closing the stopcock in the feed pipe or by laying a batten across the tank and tying the float arm to it.

The main draincock for the system will normally be in the return pipe near the boiler. Push one end of a garden hose onto its outlet and lead the other end of the hose to a gully or soakaway in the garden, then open the draincock. If you have no key for its square shank, use an adjustable spanner.

Most of the water will drain from the system, but some will be held in the radiators. To release the trapped water, start at the top of the house and carefully open the radiator bleed valves. Air will flow into the tops of the radiators, breaking the vacuum, and the water will drain out. Last of all, drain inverted pipe loops (see below).

Refilling the system

Before refilling the system, check all the draincocks and bleed valves are closed.

Restore the water supply to the feed-and-expansion tank in the loft. Filling the system will trap air in the tops of the radiators – so when full, bleed all the radiators, starting at the bottom of the house. You may also have to bleed the circulating pump. Finally, check all the draincocks and bleed valves for leaks, and tighten them if necessary.

Draincock key
A special tool is available for operating draincocks.

Cleaning the system

After installing or modifying a central-heating system, flush the pipework to get rid of swarf and flux, which can induce corrosion and damage valves or the pump.

Turn the pump impeller with a screwdriver before running the system in order to make sure it's clear. If you can feel resistance, drain the system and remove the pump before cleaning and refitting.

Descaling

If your system is old or badly corroded, a harsh cleaner or descaler may expose minor leaks sealed by corrosion – so use a mild cleanser, introduced into the system via the feed-and-expansion tank or inject it into a radiator via the bleed valve. Manufacturers' instructions vary, but in general the cleanser is left in the system for a week, with the boiler set to a fairly high temperature.

Afterwards, turn off and drain the system, then refill and drain it several times – if possible, using a hose to run mains-pressure water through the system while draining it. Some cleansers must be neutralized before you can add a corrosion inhibitor.

If your boiler is making loud banging noises, treat it with a fairly powerful descaler, running the hot-water programme only.

Draining procedure
Turn off the mains supply to the tank at the feed-pipe stopcock (**1**). If there's no stopcock, tie the float-valve arm to a batten laid across the tank (**2**). With a hose pushed onto the main draincock (**3**) and its other end at a gully or soakaway outside, open the draincock and let the system empty. Release any water trapped in the radiators (**4**) by opening their bleed valves (**5**), starting at the top of the house. Be sure to close all draincocks before you refill the system.

• **Power-flushing the system**
After upgrading an older system, perhaps with a new boiler or radiators, you could flush the system yourself (see left), but it's advisable to have it cleansed thoroughly by a heating engineer, using a power-flushing unit. When it is connected, the unit pumps chemically-treated water through the system to flush out impurities.

Inverted pipe loops

Often when fitting a central-heating system in a house that has a solid ground floor, installers run the heating pipes from the boiler into the ceiling void and drop them down the walls to the individual radiators. These 'inverted pipe loops' have their own draincock and must be drained separately after the main system has been emptied.

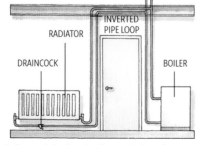

An inverted pipe loop has its own draincock

SEE ALSO > Turning off the water 40, Bleeding radiators 65

Maintaining your boiler

Oil-fired and gas boilers must be serviced annually to work efficiently and this work must be carried out by a qualified engineer. With either type of boiler, you can enter into a contract for regular maintenance with your fuel supplier or the original installer.

Corrosion in the system

- **Servicing gas boilers**
Any maintenance that involves dismantling any part of a gas boiler must be carried out by a CORGI-registered engineer, who should undertake all the necessary gas-safety checks as part of the service. There's no point in attempting to service the boiler yourself if you are not qualified and equipped to do so – it can also be dangerous, and you will be breaking the law.

Modern boilers and radiators are made from fairly thin materials, and if you fail to take basic anti-corrosion measures, the life of the system can be reduced to 10 years or less. Corrosion may result either from hard-water deposits or from a chemical reaction between the water and the system's metal components.

Lime scale
Scale builds up quickly in hard-water areas of the country. Even a thin layer of lime scale on the inner wall of a boiler's heat exchanger reduces its efficiency and may cause banging and knocking within the system. In fact, the scale can insulate sections of the heat exchanger to such an extent that it produces 'hot spots', leading to premature failure of the component.

Reducing corrosion

Drain about 600ml (1 pint) of water from the boiler or a radiator. Orange water denotes rusting, and black the presence of sludge. In either case, treat immediately with corrosion inhibitor (see below).

If there are no obvious signs of corrosion, test for inhibitor levels by dropping two plain steel nails into a jar containing some water from the system, and place two similar nails in a jar of clean tap water. After a few days the nails in the tap water should rust; but if the system contains sufficient corrosion inhibitor, the nails in the system water will remain bright – if they don't, your system needs topping up with inhibitor. It is important to use the same product that is already present in the system – if you don't know what that is, drain and flush the system, then refill with fresh water and inhibitor.

Adding corrosion inhibitor
You can slow down corrosion by adding a proprietary corrosion inhibitor to the water. This is best done when the system is first installed – but the inhibitor can be introduced into the system at any time,

Rust
Rust corrodes steel components, most notably radiators. Most rusting occurs within weeks of filling the system; but if air is being sucked in constantly, then rusting is progressive. Having to bleed radiators regularly is a sure sign that air is being drawn into the system.

Sludge
Magnetite (black sludge) clogs the pump and builds up in the bottom of radiators, reducing their heat output.

Electrolytic action
Dissimilar metals, such as copper and aluminium, act like a battery in the acidic water that is present in some central-heating systems. This results in corrosion.

provided the boiler is descaled before doing so. If the system has been running for some time, it is better to flush it out first by draining and refilling it repeatedly until the water runs clean. Otherwise, drain off about 20 litres (4 gallons) of water – enough to empty the feed-and-expansion tank and a small amount of pipework – then pour the inhibitor into the tank and restore the water supply, which will carry the inhibitor into the pipes. About 5 litres (1 gallon) will be enough for most systems, but check the manufacturer's instructions. Finally, switch on the pump to distribute the inhibitor throughout the system.

Reducing scale
You can buy low-voltage coils to create a magnetic field that will prevent the heat exchanger of your boiler becoming coated with scale. However, unless you have soft water in your area, the only way to actually avoid hard water in the system is to install a water softener.

Before fitting any device to reduce scale, it is essential to seek the boiler manufacturer's advice.

Locating gas boilers
Modern boilers fit snugly into standard kitchen cupboards.

Servicing schemes

It pays to have your central-heating system serviced regularly. Check the Yellow Pages for a suitable engineer, or ask the original installer of the system if they are willing to undertake the necessary servicing.

Gas installations
Gas suppliers offer a choice of servicing schemes for boilers, primarily provided to cover their own installations, but they will also service systems put in by other installers following a satisfactory inspection of the installation.

The simplest of the schemes provides for an annual check and adjustment of the boiler. If any repairs are found to be necessary, either at the time of the regular check or at other times during the year, then the labour and necessary parts are charged separately. But for an extra fee it is possible to have both free labour and free parts for boiler repairs at any time of year. The gas supplier will also extend the arrangement to include inspection of the whole heating system when the boiler is being checked, plus free parts and labour for repairs.

You may find that your installer or a local firm of CORGI heating engineers offers a similar choice of servicing and maintenance contracts.

Oil-fired installations
Installers of oil-fired central-heating systems and suppliers of fuel oil offer servicing and maintenance contracts similar to those outlined above for gas-fired systems. The choice of schemes available ranges from an annual check-up to complete cover for parts and labour whenever repairs are necessary.

As with the schemes for gas, it pays to shop around and make a comparison of the various services on offer and the charges that apply.

Solid-fuel systems
If you have a solid-fuel system, it is important to have the chimney and the flueway swept twice a year. The job is very similar to sweeping an open-fire chimney, access being either through the front of a room heater that has a back boiler or through a soot door in the flue pipe or chimney breast.

Once the chimney has been swept, clean out the boiler with a stiff brush, remove the dust and soot, lift out any broken fire bars and drop new ones in.

SEE ALSO ▸ Grants 7, Central-heating boilers 58, Flushing the system 63

System repairs and maintenance

Trapped air prevents radiators from heating up fully, and a regular intake of air can cause corrosion. If a radiator feels cooler at the top than at the bottom, it's likely that a pocket of air has formed inside it and is impeding full circulation of the water. Getting the air out of a radiator – 'bleeding' it – is a simple procedure.

Bleeding a radiator

First switch off the circulation pump, otherwise it may suck air into the radiator when a bleed valve is opened.

Each radiator has a bleed valve at one of its top corners, identifiable by a square-section shank in the centre of the round blanking plug. If you don't have a key, they are readily available from any DIY shop or ironmongers. Some valves are simply opened with a screwdriver.

Use the key to turn the valve's shank anticlockwise about a quarter of a turn. It shouldn't be necessary to turn it further – but have a small container handy to catch spurting water, in case you open the valve too far. You will probably also need a rag to mop up water that dribbles from the valve and it's wise to protect carpets in case of a spill. Don't try to speed up the process by opening the valve further than necessary to let the air out – that is likely to produce a deluge of water.

You will hear a hissing sound as the air escapes. Keep the key on the shank of the valve and when the hissing stops and the first dribble of water appears, close the valve tightly.

Fitting an air separator

If you are having to bleed a radiator or radiators frequently, a large quantity of air is entering the system, which can lead to serious corrosion.

Check that the feed-and-expansion tank in the loft is not acting like a radiator and warming up when you run the central heating or hot water. This indicates that hot water is being pumped through the vent pipe into the tank and taking air with it back into the system. Fit an air separator in the vent pipe, linked to the cold feed from the feed-and-expansion tank.

If the pump is fitted on the boiler return pipe, it may be sucking in air through the unions or through leaking valve spindles.

Heating system with air separator
1 Cold-water storage tank
2 Feed-and-expansion tank
3 Air separator
4 Pump
5 Motorized valve
6 Hot-water cylinder
7 Boiler
8 Radiator flow
9 Radiator return

Blocked bleed valve

If no water or air comes out when you attempt to bleed a radiator, check whether the feed-and-expansion tank in the loft is empty. If the tank is full of water, then the bleed valve is probably blocked with paint.

Close the inlet and outlet valve at each end of the radiator, then remove the screw from the centre of the bleed valve. Clear the hole with a piece of wire, and reopen one of the radiator valves slightly to eject some water from the hole. Close the radiator valve again and refit the screw in the bleed valve. Open both radiator valves and test the bleed valve again.

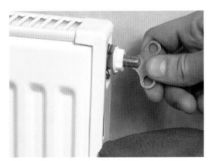

Dispersing an air pocket in a radiator

Removing a radiator

If a radiator won't warm up and you suspect it could be partially blocked with corrosion, take it outside so you can flush out the debris. You can remove individual radiators without having to drain the whole system.

Make sure you have plenty of rag to hand for mopping up spilled water, plus a jug and a large bowl. The water in the radiator may be very dirty – so roll back the floorcovering before you start.

Shut off both valves, turning the shank of the lockshield valve clockwise with a key or an adjustable spanner (**1**). Note the number of turns needed to close it, so that later you can reopen it by the same amount.

Unscrew the cap-nut that keeps the handwheel valve or lockshield valve attached to the adaptor in the end of the radiator (**2**). Hold the jug under the joint and open the bleed valve slowly to let the water drain out. Transfer the water from the jug to the bowl, and continue until no more water can be drained off.

Unscrew the cap-nut that keeps the other valve attached to the radiator, lift the radiator free from its wall brackets, and drain any remaining water into the bowl (**3**).

After replacing the radiator, tighten the cap-nuts on both valves. Close the bleed valve and reopen both valves (open the lockshield valve by the same number of turns you used when closing it). Last of all, bleed the air from the radiator.

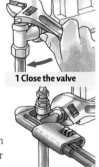

1 Close the valve

2 Unscrew cap-nut

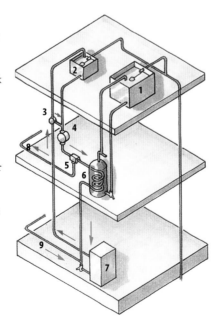

3 Lift radiator from brackets and drain

SEE ALSO > Draining the system 63, Filling the system 63

Replacing radiator valves

Like taps, radiator valves can develop leaks, although they're usually relatively easy to cure. Occasionally, however, it's necessary to replace a faulty valve or install a thermostatic valve in its place.

Curing a leaking radiator valve

Water leaking from a radiator valve is probably seeping from around the spindle (see left). However, when the water runs round and drips from the valve's cap-nut, it's the nut that often appears to be the source of the leak. Dry the valve, then hold a paper tissue against the various parts of the valve to ascertain exactly where the moisture is coming from. If the nut is leaking, tighten it gently; if that's unsuccessful, undo and reseal it (see right).

Grip leaky valve with wrench and tighten cap-nut

VALVE HEAD

SPINDLE

GLAND NUT

Leaking spindle
To stop a leak from a radiator-valve spindle, tighten the gland nut with a spanner. If the leak persists, undo the nut and wind a few turns of PTFE tape down into the spindle.

Replacing a worn or damaged valve

To replace a valve, drain the system, then lay rags under the valve to catch the dregs. Holding the body of the valve with a wrench (or water-pump pliers), use an adjustable spanner to unscrew the cap-nuts that hold the valve to the pipe (**1**) and also to the adaptor in the end of the radiator. Lift the valve from the end of the pipe (**2**); if you're replacing a lockshield valve, close it first – counting the turns, so you can open the new valve by the same number to balance the radiator.

Unscrew the valve adaptor from the radiator (**3**). You may be able to use an adjustable spanner, depending on the type of adaptor, or you may need a hexagonal radiator spanner.

Fitting the new valve
Ensure that the threads in the end of the radiator are clean. Drag the teeth of a hacksaw across the threads of the new adaptor to roughen them slightly, then wind PTFE tape four or five times around them. Screw the adaptor into the end of the radiator and tighten with a spanner.

Slide the valve cap-nut and a new olive over the end of the pipe and fit the valve (**4**) – but don't tighten the cap-nut yet. First, holding the valve body with a wrench, align it with the adaptor and tighten the cap-nut that holds them together (**5**). Then tighten the cap-nut that holds the valve to the water pipe and replace the valve head (**6**). Refill the system and check for leaks.

• **Resealing a cap-nut**
Drain the system and undo the leaking nut. Smear the olive with silicone sealant and retighten the cap-nut. Don't overtighten the nut or you may damage the olive. As an alternative to sealant, wind two turns of PTFE tape around the olive (not around the threads).

Replacing O-rings in a Belmont valve

The spindle of a Belmont valve is sealed with O-rings – which you can replace without having to drain the radiator. To find out which O-rings you need, take the plastic head of the valve to a plumbers' merchant before you begin work. On very old valves the rings are green, whereas the newer rings are red.

Undo the spindle (which has a left-hand thread). A small amount of water will leak out – but as you continue to remove the spindle, water pressure will seal the valve.

Prise off the O-rings, using a small screwdriver, and then lubricate the spindle with a smear of silicone grease. Slide on the new rings and replace the spindle.

Replacing O-rings
O-rings are housed in grooves in the valve spindle. Water pressure will seal the valve as the spindle is removed.

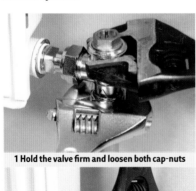

1 Hold the valve firm and loosen both cap-nuts

2 Unscrew the cap-nuts and lift the valve out

3 Remove the valve adaptor from the radiator

4 Fit new adaptor, then fit the new valve

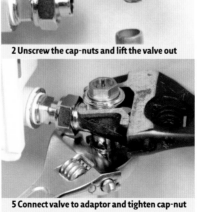

5 Connect valve to adaptor and tighten cap-nut

6 Replace the valve head

SEE ALSO > Grants 7, Thermostatic valves 61, Draining the system 63, Refilling the system 63

Underfloor heating

Thanks to flexible plastic plumbing, sophisticated controls and efficient insulation, underfloor heating is becoming a more popular and affordable form of central heating. Most systems are installed as the house is being built, but specialist manufacturers have developed a range of warm-water heating systems to suit virtually any situation.

Underfloor-heating systems

Underfloor heating can be incorporated into any type of floor construction, including solid-concrete floors, boarded floating floors and suspended timber floors (see below). The heat emanates from a continuous length of plastic pipe that snakes across the floor – like an elongated radiator – across one or more rooms.

The entire floor area is divided into separate zones to provide the most efficient layout. Each zone is controlled by a roomstat and is connected to a thermostatically controlled multi-valve manifold that forms the heart of the system. The manifold controls the temperature of the water and the flow rate to the various zones. Once a room or zone reaches its required temperature, a valve automatically shuts off that part of the circuit. A flow meter for each of the zones allows the circuits to be balanced when setting up the system and subsequently monitors its performance.

The manifold, which is installed above floor level, is connected to the boiler via a conventional circulation pump.

Methods for installing underfloor heating

When underfloor heating is installed in a new building, the plastic tubes are usually set into a solid-concrete floor. Flooring insulation is laid over the base concrete, and rows of special pipe clips are fixed to the insulation; sometimes a metal mesh is used instead of the clips. The flexible heating tubes are then clipped into place at the required spacings (see opposite), and a concrete screed is poured on top.

With a boarded floating floor, a layer of grooved insulation is laid over the concrete base, and the pipes are set in aluminium 'diffusion' plates inserted in the grooves. The entire floor area is then covered with an edge-bonded chipboard or a similar decking material.

The heating pipes can be fastened with spacer clips to the underside of a suspended wooden floor. In this situation, clearance holes are drilled through the joists at strategic points to permit a continuous run of pipework. Reflective foil and thick blanket insulation is installed below the pipes.

It is possible to lay the pipes on top of a suspended floor, but this method raises the floor level by the thickness of the pipe assembly and the new decking.

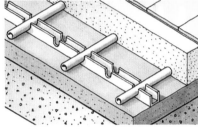
Screeded concrete floor

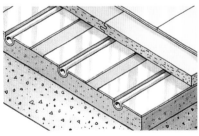
Boarded floating floor

Suspended wooden floor
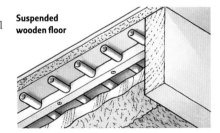

Benefits of underfloor heating

Although it's easier to incorporate underfloor heating while a house is being built, installing it in an existing building is possible, though you may have to raise floors to accommodate it. Underfloor heating can be made to work alongside a panel-radiator system and can provide the ideal solution for heating a new conservatory, for example.

Compared with panel radiators, an underfloor-heating system radiates heat more evenly and over a wider area. This has the effect of reducing hot and cold spots within the room and produces a more comfortable environment, where the air is warmest at floor level and cools as it rises towards the ceiling.

Underfloor heating is more energy-efficient and less costly to run than other central-heating systems because it operates at a lower temperature – and because there's a more even temperature throughout a room, the roomstat can be set a degree or two lower. With relatively cool water in the return cycle, a modern condensing boiler works even more efficiently.

● **Combining systems**
You can have radiators upstairs and underfloor heating downstairs. A mixing manifold will allow you to combine the two systems, using the same boiler. Any type of boiler is suitable for underfloor heating, but a condensing boiler is the most economical.

SEE ALSO > Choosing a system 56, Panel radiators 59, Thermostats 61

Installing underfloor heating

Underfloor heating is a good choice for heating a new conservatory. The large areas of glass in a conservatory present very few options for placing radiators, and the concrete slab that is typically used for conservatory floors provides an ideal base for this form of heating.

The basic plumbing system

Your supplier will suggest the best point to connect your new plumbing to the existing central-heating circuit. It can be at any convenient point, provided that the performance of your radiators will not be affected.

The pipework connecting the manifold for the underfloor heating to the radiator circuit can be metal or plastic, and it can be the same size as, but not larger than, the existing pipes. Again, your supplier will advise what to use.

The flow and return pipes from the manifold to the conservatory circuit (illustrated here, as an example) are connected to individual zone distributors, which in turn are connected to the flexible underfloor-heating tubes.

Basic system
1 Flow and return pipes from existing central-heating circuit
2 Water-temperature mixing valve
3 Pump
4 Manifold with zone valves
5 Zone distributors
6 Underfloor-heating tube

Where to start

Send details of your proposed extension to the underfloor-heating supplier. In order to be able to supply you with a well-planned scheme and quotation, the company will also need a scaled plan of your house and the basic details of your present central-heating system.

Your options

The simplest system will connect to the pipework of your existing radiator circuit. Heat for the extension will be available only when the existing central heating is running, although the temperature in the conservatory can be controlled independently by a roomstat connected to a motorized zone valve and the underfloor-heating pump.

For full control, the flow and return pipework to the underfloor system must be connected directly to the boiler, and the roomstat must be wired up to switch the boiler on and off and to control the temperature of the conservatory.

Constructing the floor

Floor construction
1 Blinded hardcore
2 DPM
3 Concrete base
4 Insulation
5 Edge insulation
6 Pipe clips and pipe
7 Screed
8 Floor tiles

You will need to excavate the site and lay a concrete base as recommended by the conservatory manufacturer, a surveyor, or your local Building Control Officer. The base must include a damp-proof membrane.

Allow for a covering layer of floor insulation – a minimum of 50mm (2in) flooring-grade expanded polystyrene or 30mm (1¼in) extruded polyurethane (check with your Building Control Officer). The floor should be finished with a 65mm (2½in) sand-and-cement screed, plus the preferred floorcovering.

When laying the floor insulation slabs, you should install a strip of insulation, 25mm (1in) thick, all round the edges. This is to prevent cold bridging between the masonry walls and the floor screed.

Cut a hole through the house wall, ready for the new plumbing that will connect to the existing central-heating system.

Installing the system

Mount the manifold in a convenient place and connect the two distributor blocks below it – one for the flow and the other for the return. Run the flow and return pipes back into the house, ready for connecting to the existing central-heating circuit. Install your new pump, and a mixing valve in both the flow pipe and the return pipe. Following the manufacturer's layout, press the spikes of the pipe clips into the insulation at the prescribed spacing (**1**). Lay out the heating tubes for both coils and clip them into place. Push the end of one of the coils into the flow distributor, and the other end of the same coil into the return distributor (**2**). Connect the other coil similarly.

Connect the flow and return pipes to the house's central-heating – it pays to insert isolating valves, so that you can shut off the new circuit for servicing. Fill, flush out and check the new system for leaks.

Apply the screed, composed of 4 parts sharp sand : 1 part cement, with a plasticizer additive. Leave it to dry naturally for at least 3 weeks before laying your floorcovering. Fit the roomstat at head height.

1 Press the pipe clips into place

2 Push tubing into the distributors

SEE ALSO > Heating controls 61, Draining the system 63

Glossary

AIRBRICK
Perforated house brick that allows air to circulate below suspended floors, in order to prevent dry rot from developing.

AIRLOCK
A blockage in a pipe caused by a trapped bubble of air.

APPLIANCE
Machine or device powered by electricity. *or* A functional piece of equipment connected to the plumbing system, such as a handbasin, sink, bathtub etc.

BACK-SIPHONING
The siphoning of part of a plumbing system caused by the failure of mains water pressure.

BALANCED FLUE
A ducting system that allows a heating appliance, such as a boiler, to draw fresh air from and discharge gases to the outside of a building.

BATT
A short cut length of glass-fibre or mineral-fibre insulant.

BATTEN
A narrow strip of wood.

BLACK WATER
Water, containing human waste, flushed from a WC. See also Grey water.

BLEED VALVE
Small screw situated at one of the top corners of a radiator. Turning the screw allows trapped air to escape, so the radiator can fill will hot water and reach its optimum temperature.

BORE
The hollow part of a pipe or tube. *or* To drill a hole.

CAP-NUT
Nut used to tighten a fitting onto pipework.

CASEMENT
The opening part of a hinged window.

CAVITY WALL
Wall made of two separate, parallel masonry skins with an air space between them.

CIRCUIT
A complete path through which an electric current can flow.

CISTERN
Container for cold water, which is drawn off as required, typically for flushing a WC.

CONDENSATION
Moisture deposited on a relatively cold surface, such as a windowpane. This is caused when water vapour in warm moist air is liquidized by the air coming into contact with the cold surface.

CONDENSING BOILER
Central-heating boiler that extracts and utilizes some of the heat from its own exhaust gases.

CONDUCTOR
A component, usually a length of wire, along which an electric current will pass.

CYLINDER
Cylindrical copper container for storing heated water.

CYLINDER FLANGE
Connection for hot-water supply from the storage cylinder. See also Essex flange and Surrey flange.

DAMP-PROOF COURSE
A layer of impervious material that prevents moisture rising from the ground into the walls of a building.

DATUM POINT
The point from which measurements are taken.

DEHUMIDIFIER
Device that extracts water vapour from the air and then warms the dry air before returning it to the room.

DRY-LINE
To cover the inner surface of a wall with plasterboard, which is sometimes insulated. The plasterboard is either nailed to strips of wood or glued directly to the wall.

EARTH
A connection between an electrical circuit and the earth (ground). *or* Terminal to which the earth connection is made.

EAVES
The edges of a roof that project beyond the walls.

ENERGY PERFORMANCE CERTIFICATE
Document that describes the energy-efficiency of a building and recommends measures to improve that energy-efficiency.

ESSEX FLANGE
Side-entry connection for the hot-water supply from a hot-water storage cylinder.

EXTENSION
A room or rooms added to an existing building.

FURRING BATTENS
See Furring strips.

FURRING STRIPS
Parallel strips of wood fixed to a wall or ceiling to provide a framework for attaching panels.

FUSE BOARD
Where the main electrical service cable is connected to the house circuitry. *or* The accumulation of consumer unit, meter etc.

GREY WATER
Water drained from handbasins, bathtubs and showers. See also Black water.

HARD WATER
Water containing a large percentage of dissolved minerals, which are deposited as lime scale inside kettles, hot-water cylinders and plumbing systems. See also Soft water.

HEAD
The height of the surface of water above a specific point, used as a measurement of pressure – for example, a head of 2m (6ft).

HEAT-RECOVERY VENTILATOR
Appliance that extracts heat from the stale air it removes from inside a building and then transfers the heat to the fresh air it draws in from outside.

INSULATION
Materials used to reduce the transmission of heat or sound. *or* Nonconductive material surrounding electrical wires or connections to prevent the passage of electricity.

JOIST
A horizontal wooden or metal beam (such as a rolled-steel joist) used to support a structure such as a floor, ceiling or wall.

LAGGING
Insulation wrapped around pipework or around a hot-water cylinder. *or* To apply insulation.

LIGHT PIPE
Tube with highly reflective inner surface that transmits daylight from roof level to an interior space.

LIME SCALE
Hard white deposits found inside plumbing and heating systems, caused by minerals dissolved in water as it passes through the ground.

NOGGING
A short horizontal wooden member between studs.

PARTY WALL
Wall between two houses over which each of the adjoining owners has equal rights in law.

PHASE
The part of an electrical circuit that carries the flow of current to an appliance or accessory. Also known as 'live'.

PROTECTIVE MULTIPLE EARTH
A system of electrical wiring in which the neutral part of the circuit is used to take earth-leakage current to earth.

RAFTER
One of a set of parallel sloping beams that form the main structural element of a roof.

RAMMED-EARTH CONSTRUCTION
Method of building walls by compacting subsoil, sometimes mixed with a binder, into purpose-built formwork. Removing the formwork reveals a strong dense wall that has good insulating properties.

RENEWABLE ENERGY
Heat or electricity that is generated by wind, waves or solar radiation, as opposed to the burning of fossil fuels.

RESIDUAL CURRENT DEVICE
A device that monitors the flow of electrical current through the live and neutral wires of a circuit. When an RCD detects an imbalance caused by earth leakage, it cuts off the supply of electricity as a safety precaution.

RISING MAIN
The pipe that supplies water under mains pressure, usually to a storage tank in the roof.

ROOF LIGHT
Window built into the sloping part of a roof. A roof light can be fixed or openable.

SANITARYWARE
Bathroom fittings, such as handbasins, bathtubs, bidets, WC pans and cisterns.

SASH
The openable part of a sliding window.

SHEATHING
The outer layer of insulation surrounding an electrical cable or flexible cord.

SHORT CIRCUIT
The accidental rerouting of electricity to earth, which increases the flow of current and blows a fuse.

SLEEPER WALL
A low masonry wall that serves as an intermediate support for ground-floor joists.

SOFFIT
The underside of part of a building, such as the underside of the eaves.

SOFT WATER
Water containing a relatively small percentage of dissolved minerals. Soft water occurs mostly in areas with dense rocky terrain, where rainwater tends to run over the surface of the ground rather than being absorbed into the soil. See also Hard water.

SOLAR ENERGY
Usable heat absorbed from sunlight falling onto collectors that are typically mounted on a south-facing slope of a roof.

SOLAR GAIN
Additional space heating acquired from sunlight falling through glazed windows.

STUD PARTITION
A timber-frame interior dividing wall.

SUSPENDED FLOOR
Wood floor constructed from stout joists overlaid by boards. A suspended floor spans the distance between all four walls of a room, leaving a clear space below.

SUSSEX FLANGE
Top-entry flange that screws into the vent-pipe connection on top of a hot-water storage cylinder. See Cylinder flange.

SUSTAINABLE
Term used to describe a material, such as timber, that has been harvested from an area that is subsequently replanted with a similar crop. The term is also used to describe energy that can be reproduced

without recourse to consuming finite stocks of fossil fuels.

SUPPLEMENTARY BONDING
The connecting to earth of electrical appliances and exposed metal pipework in a bathroom or kitchen.

TERMINAL
A connection to which the bared ends of electrical cable or flex are attached.

THERMAL BRIDGE
Area of conductive material that is able to transmit heat and bypass surrounding insulation.

THERMOSTAT
Device for regulating ambient temperature.

TRAP
A bent section of pipe below a bath, sink etc. It contains standing water to prevent the passage of gases.

TRICKLE VENT
Fixed ventilator without moving parts through which fresh air is drawn slowly into a building by natural convection.

TURBINE
Device that generates electricity, using rotational forces created by the movement of air or fluid.

VAPOUR BARRIER
A layer of impervious material that prevents the passage of moisture-laden air.

VAPOUR CHECK
See Vapour barrier.

WARM-ROOF SYSTEM
Roof construction with layers of insulation embedded within the outermost part of the structure, in order to enclose a living space, such as in the loft.

WATER HAMMER
Vibration in plumbing caused by fluctuating water pressure.

Index